TEN
GOLDEN
RULES
FOR
FINANCIAL
SUCCESS

TEN GOLDEN RULES FOR FINANCIAL SUCCESS

Gary Moore

Foreword by Sir John M. Templeton

ZondervanPublishingHouse
Grand Rapids, Michigan

A Division of HarperCollinsPublishers

Ten Golden Rules for Financial Success
Copyright © 1996 by Gary D. Moore

Requests for information should be addressed to:

ZondervanPublishingHouse
Grand Rapids, Michigan 49530

Library of Congress Cataloging-in-Publication Data

Moore, Gary D.
    Ten Golden rules for financial success : riches I've gathered from legendary mutual fund manager Sir John M. Templeton / Gary Moore.
        p. cm.
    Includes bibliographical references.
    ISBN: 0-310-20693-6
    1. Finance, Personal—Religious aspects—Christianity.   2. Templeton, John, 1912– .
I. Templeton, John, 1912– . II. Title.
HG179.M614   1996
332.6—dc20   96–8071
                                                                CIP

This edition printed on acid-free paper and meets the American National Standards Institute Z39.48 standard.

Interior design by Sue Vandenberg Koppenol

Printed in the United States of America

---

96 97 98 99 00 01 02/❖ DH/ 10 9 8 7 6 5 4 3 2

Truly a legend in our time, John Templeton understands that the real measure of a person's success in life is not financial accomplishment but moral integrity and inner character.

Billy Graham

The optimist is right. The pessimist is right. The one differs from the other as the light from the dark. Yet both are right. Each is right from his own particular point of view, and this point of view is the determining factor in the life of each. It determines whether it is a life of power or of impotence, of peace or of pain, of success or of failure.

from *In Tune with the Infinite*
(one of John Templeton's favorite books)

Contents

Foreword

In a 1994 interview with James D. Davis of the *Orlando-Sun Sentinel*, called "Prophets and Profits," I said the following: "I've found that spiritual attitudes lead to material rewards. That holds true for an individual, a corporation or a nation. I could write a book about it."

I was gratified when Gary Moore suggested he would write that very book. Since I sold my mutual-fund business a few years ago, I have devoted 100% of my time to several projects dedicated to spiritual advancement worldwide. So my time has been limited.

My agreement with Gary was that I would make no suggestions or have any direct say in what he wrote. I have simply checked the quotes attributed to me to assure their accuracy. I would note, however, that while I have made many mistakes over the years, Gary has obviously thought that what I have done successfully might be of some use to others.

The absence of my direct involvement in this work should not discourage you. A few years ago, Gary spoke to the 16,000-member Willow Creek Church outside Chicago. They taped his seminar. As he had discussed some of my ideas, he was good enough to forward one of the tapes to me. I ordered several for friends. The gentleman who introduced Gary said this:

> Gary Moore has professional credentials that put him in a world class. He was a senior vice president of Paine Webber. He is a UPI commentator and syndicated columnist. He has authored an outstanding book. He takes you deep and profoundly into a Christian understanding of money. He is also investment counselor to some of the best-known banks, churches and individuals in America. He is a profound thinker. But for me, perhaps even more important, he is a profoundly dedicated Christian, a sensitive servant, who has a passion for helping folks understand at a deeper level the biblical implications of stewardship.

May God bless you.

Sir John M. Templeton

Dedication

In addition to my loving wife and son, who paid more than the usual price as I took another year of our life together to write another manuscript, I dedicate this book to:

Lee—a deeply religious woman who attended a Christian financial conference in late 1994. She returned believing she had only a few days to shift all her investments into treasury bills as protection against a financial collapse, which she had been assured was imminent. You missed a golden opportunity to prosper in 1995, when stocks and bonds soared to record levels. Have faith that you will have another chance.

I also dedicate this book to Andy, a highly successful and respected businessman who told me recently that he studies the lives of five Americans. As he named them, I sadly noted that each was dead. When I asked him to name one living person he would like his child to emulate, he said he couldn't. Have faith that such people exist.

I dedicate this book to the surprising number of friends—wonderful friends within our churches, religious media, and publishing houses—who have recently told me they now call themselves "followers of Jesus" rather than "Christians." Have faith that the old term is too rich in both tradition and promise to be discarded as we pursue success.

I dedicate this book to my dear friend Frank, who told me recently that he was afraid the future did not look promising for his sons. But he couldn't give me a reason. Have faith that our fathers achieved success by fearing nothing but fear itself.

I dedicate this book to Ann Spangler and Bob Hudson, my editors. I have discovered that being an author is like being a pastor—except I only get to preach every few years. Therefore, we authors can become over-passionate when we finally get our chance. The job of a good editor is to ensure our enthusiasm doesn't empty the church before people hear the entire message. I'm grateful that Ann and Bob have crafted a book that may inspire you to new heights of understanding and achievement, rather than inspiring you out the front door. Have faith that there are enriching concepts within. We are confused, worried and afraid. But we are loved.

Finally, I dedicate this book, with great love, to Kathryn, my mother. There were surely times you worried that I had forgotten the lessons you taught in our rambling country home and our tiny country church. But your ultimate faith in "train up a child . . ." appears justified. I am beginning to remember, and truly believe, those stories from my youth.

Introduction:
Keep the Faith

> The beginning of anxiety is the end of faith, and the beginning
> of true faith is the end of anxiety.
>
> George Müller

Although we moderns often associate ancient prophets like Jeremiah with gloomy foreboding about the future, I wonder if they haven't been the subject of bad press. Indeed, Jeremiah spent much of his time urging his contemporaries to remember forgotten virtues. In that, he was much like our modern "virtuecrats," such moral leaders as Bill Bennett, Peggy Noonan, and Bill Kristol.

But another dimension of the ancient prophets is too often overlooked. They were profoundly hopeful people. If our modern prophets fall short, it may be in this. Reflect on the rich promises contained in these words: "'I know the plans I have for you,' declares the LORD, 'plans to prosper you and not to harm you, plans to give you hope and a future'" (Jeremiah 29:11). Jeremiah wrote these words to a nation beginning an exile in a hostile land that would continue for seven decades. One can only guess the skepticism of those who heard his counsel.

Things are not so different today. For seven decades, Americans of wavering faith have lived in a land increasingly shaped by secular humanism. Many of us have devoted our lives to the pursuit of material riches and discovered that, as important as these riches seem, making them priority always leads to pessimism. The ancients could have told us: we never have enough money to make us happy. Others of us place our faith in human leaders, both political and corporate, a pursuit that also leads to disappointment and more pessimism.

So, as we survey our misplaced priorities and misplaced faith, it is easy to lose hope—and we have no shortage of prophets to affirm our sense of hopelessness with their visions of doom. Yet amid these voices, one—Sir John Templeton's—has consistently offered hope. He has quietly encouraged us to remember the ancient virtues: Attend to your business, give and save; have faith that God loves you and plans good things for your future; and trust that people will eventually seek the God who alone can provide an abundant life.

Many of us will be skeptical of that counsel. And not so long ago, I was too. But you will hear more about that in due time.

For now, note that the *Wall Street Journal* recently said: "The relationship between wealth and religion is becoming a hot topic . . ." As I read it, I felt I was standing beside Noah on the deck of the ancient ark, watching the dove return with the olive branch. In essence, you'll soon realize that most of us have been content to keep God in heaven while we've left our world to be managed by human politicians, journalists and economists. As we approach a new millennium, that sentence may be a sign of hope that this flood of humanism may finally be receding.

The book you are about to read contains three lessons:

First, it will tell you the good things that have been happening in our political economy in recent years—things that the politicians, pundits, and self-proclaimed prophets may not have mentioned.

Second, it will offer advice about your personal finances.

Third, it will, I hope, renew your hope in the future and in the good things that it may hold for you and your children.

These three lessons are couched in Ten Golden Rules. The first three rules comprise the first lesson. They provide many economic facts that far too many leaders have neglected to share in recent years, though you will discover they are terribly important. In the Information Age, your success will increasingly depend on your developing your own perspective of the political economy, rather than depending on others of various political and financial motives to develop it for you. In my first book, *The Christian's Guide to Wise Investing,* I focused exclusively on teaching people how to navigate the world of personal financial management and investments, all of which, I have learned, is of little use when we have been taught that the economic waters are too full of sharks for us to venture offshore. Golden Rules One through Three will help you understand the depths and currents of our economy. Then you can choose your own course to sail into the future.

Golden Rules Four through Eight will explain the practical aspects of trimming the sails of your own financial ship. I know this is a major reason you purchased the book. I don't think you will be disappointed. These chapters expand on what I call the "10–20–40–500 Rule." It says that if you can earn 10% on your money, save $20 a week, for 40 years, you will retire with about $500,000. For each additional 2% you earn, your accumulation will just about double (Sir John actually averaged almost 15% during the past forty years). Furthermore, I will advise you how this can be done with prudent and ethical techniques. They will make your journey smoother and more meaningful.

What you and your children can expect in the third millennium—and the obstacles that might impede our progress—is mapped out in Golden Rules Nine and Ten.

Each of these Golden Rules I have learned from studying the life and work of Sir John Templeton, so his name—and spirit—are invoked on nearly every page of this book. These Ten Golden Rules do not amount to a biography of Templeton; they are a study of how he has achieved success, in the fullest sense of the word, by integrating his beliefs with his daily life as a money manager. Templeton's philosophy is a gentle but dramatic reminder that true financial success is dependent upon the humble search for Truth—with a capital T—which penetrates the heart, plumbs the depths of the soul, and challenges the mind with difficult questions.

You will notice that I quote extensively from the great thinkers of the past and present rather than simply sharing my own perceptions of our world. This openness to the opinions of others is an enriching technique that I have learned from Templeton's own writings. Like most inexperienced counselors and investors, I had to learn this humble approach the hard way. There was a time during the late seventies when I thought I knew everything there was to know about our economy and managing money; but by the mid-eighties, I found myself starting to flee Wall Street in the direction of seminary. My flight was largely motivated by the fact I no longer knew what, or who, to believe.

The ancient Greeks believed you could predict a person's future by looking at that person's role model. Accordingly, all those who aspired to the seminary were asked about the person they had chosen to emulate in their professional careers. I replied, "John Templeton." I explained that I had lost my father too early in life and that John

Templeton had helped to fill the void. That was when I first realized that I was increasingly turning to Sir John in an effort to make some sense of my world. That process only deepened after I decided to stay in investment counseling.

When I first told that story to Sir John years later, he quietly sighed, "Oh, no." Yet I share it with you because it colors the rest of the book. In my first draft, I referred to him solely as "Sir John," which my editor warned me would strike the reader as monotonous, or even pretentious. I understand. But just as I would never have called my father "Charles" or "Moore," I am equally uncomfortable calling John Templeton anything but "Sir John," which is the term used by most of us who know and respect him. In any case, I have agreed with my editor to keep such references to a minimum. Also be assured that I have no intent to bestow sainthood on Sir John. If there is always a future for every sinner, there is also surely a past for every saint. Though he shows many outstanding human qualities, I have had my share of disagreements with him. Still, I value the lessons he has taught me about life.

Nor should you expect this book to be a hard-hitting exposé of one of the world's wealthiest and most influential men. America has seen too many exposés since the days of Watergate, which may be one reason we have such a hard time finding contemporary role models. I write, instead, out of respect for Sir John—and out of friendship—rather than adulation.

As an author and investment counselor, I have found the following Ten Golden Rules to be richly rewarding. I wrote them with my heart and soul as well as with my mind. My fondest wish is that you might be equally rewarded as you reflect on them.

As you journey through this book, visualize it as a journey through the rest of your life. As you reach each milepost—when fears return, disappointments arise, or doubts seem to overwhelm you—then meditate on these words from Thomas Edison:

> My message to you is to be courageous. I have lived a long time. I have seen history repeat itself again and again. I have seen many depressions in business. Always America has come out stronger and more prosperous. Be as brave as your fathers before you. Have faith—go forward.

one

PESSIMISM
IS NOT A VIRTUE

Surely you desire truth in the inner parts; you teach me wisdom in the inmost place.

(Psalm 51:6)

The new century, not unlike all other centuries, will provide plenty of reasons for pessimism if you start to look for them. But ultimately, pessimism is a snare and a delusion. Yes, there will be problems to confront, but there will also be new opportunities to seize; in fact, the new century will be resplendent with opportunity. . . . We are still the richest society in the history of mankind. In the new century, we can, and should choose optimism over pessimism. The danger of pessimism is that it is likely to be self-fulfilling.

Robert L. Bartley, editor, *The Wall Street Journal*

The autumn of 1982 was supposed to have witnessed the economic downfall of America. The nation's best-selling book at the time was Doug Casey's *Crisis Investing: Opportunities and Profits in the Coming Great Depression*. A prominent politician

17

endorsed the book by writing a foreword in which he immodestly stated, "A hundred years from now, should mankind survive that long, Doug Casey may well be remembered as one of the great prophets of our time." Even the cover confidently anointed the book as the "ultimate investment book."

Why was Casey considered a prophet? Economic pessimism! At one point in the book, Casey states,

> It is now virtually certain that the United States will enter a depression far greater in scope and dimension than that of the 1930s, probably by 1983 at the latest. . . . The true price of gold should be at least $3,300 an ounce. . . . The Dow Jones Industrial Average will fall to at least 300 in the not too distant future.

Yet within months the prophesy proved false. To the disbelief of tens of millions who—like Casey—had lost hope for our political economy, the Dow Jones Industrial Average actually broke the 1000 level.

Nor was Casey alone. The early eighties saw other prophets of doom pass through our land. Howard Ruff's *How to Prosper During the Coming Bad Years* spent six months at the top of the best-seller list. Among other things, Ruff predicted

> a probable downturn this year that may become a full-scale inflationary depression . . . a falling Dow Jones . . . interest rates will exceed 40% . . . Social Security pension benefits will exceed $100,000 a year—and still not be enough to live on . . . inflation will cause a Constitutional crisis before 1987.

In 1982 I had been an investment counselor for only a few years, so when the publisher of my local paper asked me where the stock market was headed, I was hardly surprised by his laughter when I replied, "Perhaps 3000 by 1990." But he stopped chuckling as soon as I said, "Sir John Templeton thinks so too."

Such is the respect people have for John Templeton—a Tennessee boy of modest circumstances who became a Phi Beta Kappa graduate of Yale in economics, a Rhodes scholar at Oxford, and an investment legend—that the newspaper actually published my thoughts about the Dow. At the same time I learned a valuable lesson about hopeful economic forecasts when I lost several clients who thought I had lost my mind. Nevertheless, my comments also enriched a few investors who had more hopeful natures.

WHAT TO BELIEVE?

*In investment work you can't afford to be an optimist or pessimist. If
you are going to succeed you need to be a realist.*

Sir John M. Templeton

By the early eighties, John Templeton had already helped countless investors prosper through decades of war, inflation, and fluctuat-
ing federal debt. His Templeton Growth Fund was, and continues to
be, the best-performing mutual fund in the world in the last half of the
twentieth century, a performance that has earned Templeton a char-
ter membership to the hall of fame on the popular television program
Wall Street Week with Louis Rukeyser. It was on Rukeyser's show of June
18, 1982—when the Dow stood at 790—that John startled Wall Street
by challenging the prophets of doom with his prediction that the Dow
would reach 3000. Eight years later, it reached that mark.

Yet even as the stock market soared to the levels John had projected, Ravi Batra's book *The Great Depression of 1990* became the new
"Monumental #1 *New York Times* Best Seller" with its thesis that "we
are ripe for economic disaster." By contrast, John wrote, "The doom-
sayer misses the overriding fact that there is a Creator behind this
drama, moving our world and us to bring an ever greater revelation of
His goodness and concern for his creation." He maintained that America was quite possibly entering the twenty most prosperous years in the
history of the world. He wrote:

> There will, of course, be corrections, perhaps even crashes. But
> over time our studies indicate stocks do go up . . . and up . . . and up.
> With the fall of communism and the sharply reduced threat of nuclear
> war, it appears that the U.S. and some form of an economically united
> Europe may be about to enter the most glorious period in their his-
> tory. . . . Business is likely to boom. Wealth will increase. . . . By the
> time the 21st century begins—it's just around the corner, you know—
> I think there is at least an even chance that the Dow Jones Industrial
> Average may have reached 6000, perhaps more. Despite all the cur-
> rent gloom about the economy and about the future, more people will
> have more money than ever before in history.[1]

Then Desert Storm blew in, and Armageddon-style books blew
back onto the best-seller lists. If any one thing keeps people from investing for the future, it is the notion there may not be one. The catch

phrase "The economy, stupid" rang true enough to put a new president in the White House. Yet through all the pessimism and politics, John quietly said he was investing more money in the stocks of American companies than at any time in his fifty years of investment counseling.

Despite the widespread pessimism, John believed the early nineties were the final stages of the mildest recession America had experienced in the post-war period and that investors were at a historical turning point that would allow them to create a world more prosperous than it had ever been.

Still, the anxieties caused by the recession and America's transition to a peacetime economy prompted the *Economist* magazine to publish an article called: "Sam, Sam, The Paranoid Man" that argued:

> When Americans look at their economy these days, they are horrified by what they see, or think they see. Economic paranoia has become an American habit. America worries as it prospers. So be it. The trouble is that in recent months these fears have become so intense they threaten to do real, not imaginary harm. Confusion is helping to feed the present mood of despair. These fears are based on false premises and are greatly overdone.[2]

Most recently this pervasive cultural paranoia canonized Harry Figgie's best-seller about the federal debt, *Bankruptcy 1995*, as the revised gospel of doom.

Pessimism and Future Success

Recently author and media critic Michael Medved spoke at Hillsdale College. The December 1995 edition of its monthly publication, *Imprimis*, shared these thoughts from his talk:

> In recent years, our nation has been torn by fears that immigrants may be bad for America. In April of 1995, however, a major study at the University of Chicago suggested the profoundly depressing possibility that the reverse could be true: America just might be bad for immigrants. Researchers surveyed more than 25,000 eighth graders and found that, in every ethnic group, children with immigrant parents perform significantly better in school than those whose parents were born here.

The defining difference, the Chicago report concluded, is "the hopeful attitude of the immigrant parents." Ironically, the longer immigrants live in this society and adjust to contemporary American norms, the more likely it is that they will lose this optimism—and their chances for success suffer accordingly.

Our children stand to lose a great deal from prolonged exposure to the dysfunctional elements of our current culture. They lose faith. They lose confidence. And they lose resistance to the most deadly epidemic menacing our youth today—which isn't AIDS, or gang violence, or teen pregnancy—but the plague of pessimism that has infected tens of millions of young Americans.

This depressed and nihilistic attitude toward life could be the biggest threat to America today. . . . Human beings will not learn, will not grow, and will not develop good character traits if they believe that discipline and hard work are pointless, that life is meaningless and unfair, and that the outlook for the future is grim.*

Some writers have even raised this paranoia to the level of Christian prophecy. Pat Robertson wrote about his visions of a possible stock market crash for 1993 in his newsletter for viewers of his television show. My friend Larry Burkett's book *The Coming Economic Earthquake* was named the book-of-the-year by religious booksellers in 1992. In another newsletter for television viewers, D. James Kennedy later wrote that our federal debt might rise almost three times higher than any serious economist had projected, and Kennedy predicted a "terrible financial holocaust" might soon plague America. Furthermore, just days before the 1994 election, televangelist John Ankerberg promoted a video entitled *The Crash: The Coming Financial Collapse of America*, which maintained that "we're going to have an economic collapse . . . that could make the depression of 1929 look like a mild recession by comparison."

Apparently, religion is doing little to heal our economic anxieties and give us hope for the future. While religious leaders obviously haven't created these anxieties, they often either ignore them or affirm them by allowing them to fester deep in our national soul, and in doing

---

*You can subscribe to *Imprimis* free of charge by calling 1-800-437-2268.

so, the church fails to be the true spiritual and countercultural power it should be.

For example, just days after Ankerberg's video appeared, a group of international businessmen voted the U.S. economy the most healthily competitive on earth and said it would remain so well into the next century; yet to my knowledge, not a single televangelist shared this good news with their flock. One year later, another survey came to the same conclusions. The *Economist* noted that American business leaders were so pessimistic that their state of mind could only be described as "deep inside the angst zone."

WEALTH WITHOUT ANXIETY

We will all gain greater perspective and greater peace if we remember something simple and difficult: We must live in the Kingdom of God and not in the world. The world is around us with all its pleasures, joys and temptations, but there is no peace there. The only peace is in the Kingdom of God, which is not far away on a map, but within you.

Peggy Noonan

During this decade of what is sometimes called "the age of anxiety," the Dow has actually doubled—just as John Templeton had predicted. Templeton, who has been called "one of the authentic heroes of Wall Street," "the greatest layman of the Christian Church in our time" (according to Norman Vincent Peale), and "truly a legend" (according to Billy Graham), has continued to spread hope through many articles and in his appearances on television shows like *Wall Street Week*. That hope has enriched him and countless others.

Templeton has lived free of the fear and anxiety that have shackled tens of millions of Americans. As the spirit of fear gradually gives way to the spirit of greed, he will live free of it as well. While it may be tempting to assume that he is free of anxiety because he is very prosperous, the truth is this: he is prosperous because he is free of anxiety. Anxiety-prone people are not likely to literally explore the world in a near penniless condition, yet that is exactly what John did after graduating from college during the Great Depression. The confidence that he gained from those travels undoubtedly prepared him for future success—and it probably contributed to his being called "the dean of global investing."

Have you ever noticed that when the Scriptures describe human encounters with the divine—as when the angels announced the birth of Jesus to the less-than-affluent shepherds—the encounter often begins with the words "Be not afraid"?

Such spiritual freedom from anxiety has many dimensions. It is built on a foundation of reasoned hopefulness, which counts blessings not often enumerated by the popular media. It gratefully acknowledges that our nation has not only collective liabilities but collective assets as well. It challenges us to move beyond our individual fears rather than affirming them. It lovingly believes in the inherent, though admittedly imperfect, decency of our fellow human beings. It obediently recognizes our great blessings and liberties, and uses them wisely. It has a humble faith in a Power that over the millennia has proven itself to be infinitely greater than our frail human efforts toward prosperity.

Perhaps most importantly, this freedom from anxiety keeps a treasury of enriching memories from long ago. It remembers how an entire nation once, thousands of years ago, dreamed of finding a "Promised Land." The people journeyed through the desert, right to the borders of that land—and then stopped. Despite divine promises, they wanted human assurances. So twelve leaders ventured forth and returned with the news that the land was indeed rich, and yet, they said, the riches were guarded by giants. Two of the men said these obstacles could be overcome. They were almost stoned for their hopeful realism. The other ten simply affirmed the worst fears of the people, and so, without ever encountering a giant, they continued to wander aimlessly in the desert, never experiencing the milk and honey of the Promised Land.

Since then, many nations and individuals have stood on the border of the Promised Land and tried to ascertain the future, but for every two leaders who have encouraged them to enter the land through faith in divine love, ten others have affirmed their worst fears. That ratio is just about the same today—even among religious leaders.[3]

This story must have been forgotten by one potential client who was referred to me several years ago. He was a businessman who also served as an associate pastor at his church. When he asked me how he might gainfully employ a fairly substantial amount of money, I suggested that he invest in a diversified portfolio of conservative stocks, bonds, and certificates of deposit, all of which would both meet his ethical criteria and create wealth around the world. He looked surprised.

He told me he had just attended a financial conference at which the keynote speaker, one of the country's leading prophets of doom-and-gloom economics, had recommended that everyone buy gold coins and international gold funds to prepare for the worst. The speaker must have been convincing, for instead of taking my advice, my potential client traded his money for gold coins, which he piled in a lockbox.

I lost touch with him shortly after that, but I heard that he was thinking of selling his business and home so he could move to a remote mountaintop retreat where he would wait for the inevitable economic collapse. I wondered how all of this was going to improve our economy for him or his children.

Then, about two years later, he called me again. He said that he and his wife had not only missed their chance to make significant returns on their money but they had experienced two of the most anxiety-filled years of their lives. Then, with an insight I rarely come across—even among pastors—he said that he was a living example of the fearful steward in the biblical parable of the talents (Matthew 25:14–30).

This ancient story, you will recall, concerns a man who fearfully hoarded the money that his master had asked him to take care of. Unlike two other servants who were entrusted with part of the master's wealth, this man buried his share in the ground instead of investing it wisely and earning a return. When the master returned after a long absence and discovered his wealth had not been used productively, the man was chastised and the money was taken from him and given to one of the other servants to invest.

As we near the end of the millennium, it seems a good time to ask why so many Americans—who are more economically blessed than any people in history—are so filled with anxiety. Our political economy cannot be any more troubled than Israel's was when Jesus taught that his followers should observe the birds of the air who live in God's loving care without fear and anxiety. He said, "Seek his kingdom, and these things will be given to you as well" (Luke 12:31). He is apparently suggesting that economic and social growth are more likely to occur when our hearts and minds are free of the spiritual confusion brought on by temporal worries. Yet many of us have turned his counsel upside down. We often think we will feel better only when we have set aside enough money and put the right person in the White House. The opposite is true, however. We are more likely to find economic sufficiency and elect wise officials when we are at peace with God and seeking his kingdom first.

MORAL AND SPIRITUAL FOUNDATIONS OF SUCCESS

What if conventional wisdom is wrong? The hardiness of voter dis-gruntlement, despite vigorous economic growth and diminishing unemploy-ment, has been a puzzle for sometime. Rising consumer confidence has coin-cided with growing grumpiness. The closer you look at what is actually happening to the economy, the deeper the puzzle—and the clearer the need to question common assumptions about the causes of discontent. . . . The greater unease may be over social and moral issues rather than the economy.

The Economist (January 28, 1995)

John Templeton once wrote, "Basic biblical and spiritual principles are the foundations for success in any endeavor. The material success is temporary, but it comes more often from being in tune with the infi-nite."[4] Before he retired, he was noted for beginning every analyst and shareholder meeting with prayer—not that he believes prayer will make his stock values rise, but he does believe prayer clears his mind of anxiety and confusion for its highest use. And his counsel that "prayer is about listening to God rather than talking to God" is a gem.

Having a spiritual foundation also gives him a clearer understand-ing of what money is for, as evidenced by his appearance on the tele-vision show *Lifestyles of the Rich and Famous*. With strains of "Amazing Grace" echoing in the background, he explained that he has never used his considerable blessings to collect yachts, planes, and other toys. There are, he believes, wiser uses for money.

John chuckled when I once described him as "a joyful John Calvin." Calvin, the founder of the Presbyterian Church to which John belongs, was a thrifty and devout man who could sometimes be stern and puri-tanical. Calvin once wrote that we should all "be instructed in the tem-poral realm largely by reason, tradition, and the authority of the great minds of the past, and in the spiritual realm by the Word of God." John seems to have found joy in this open-minded approach.

Yet it is difficult to "be instructed" when we are unwilling to exam-ine our irrational prejudices. An unwavering certainty of belief, of course, can be a theological advantage in a world of moral relativism, but stub-born adherence to questionable theories about political economy—of the kind held by many conservative religious people I work with—can be devastating in the ebb and flow of personal financial management.

This was graphically demonstrated when one of my favorite min-isters—who often counsels ministers and business professionals to seek out those who can guide us and keep us on track in our thinking—opened his best-selling doom-and-gloom economic book of the early nineties with these words: "Several of my closest friends counseled me not to write [this book]." Hundreds of thousands of people, who turned it into a best-seller, are probably wishing that he had been less certain of his economic beliefs and listened to his friends. And I wish they all had listened to John Templeton who said the same year that the odds of a 1930s-style depression was "almost zero."

WHAT IS TRUTH?

In public discussion, in the press, and in politics, theories and findings are adopted not to facilitate the search for truth but because they lead to certain policy conclusions. Theories and findings become weapons in a propaganda battle.

R. H. Coase

Of course, that assumes they had access to what John Templeton was saying at the time—which is a very large assumption. The typical American is diverted and shielded from the truth about our economy in an enormous variety of ways.

A couple of years ago, for example, John and I were asked to participate in an "economic" special for a major television ministry, which was to air just before congressional elections. The producer of the show, as soon became evident, had been influenced by some of the leading—and consistently wrong—pessimists, who were also represented on the show. After hours of filming John's and my upbeat opinions about the economy, the producer said she no longer knew what or who to believe. She said she must be struggling with the ancient question "What is truth?"

At that point, I shared this simple observation: "The interesting thing about truth is that it's never wrong." That, in fact, has been the test of prophets since the beginning of time: if their dire predictions never come to pass, you should heed their counsel with caution. If their predictions come true, as Templeton's have, then pay close attention.

When the special finally aired, however, it portrayed almost entirely the pessimistic view and shared virtually nothing of John's infectious hope. Not that the show was a complete failure. From a political standpoint, the show wisely encouraged viewers to plan on asking less of Washington in future years. But from a financial perspective, it failed to encourage Americans to invest in their future success. It wrongly encouraged the hoarding of Treasury bills and gold coins, and if any viewers actually bought into the implications of the show, they were sure to have missed investing in the explosively profitable markets of the following year. Being politically correct but financially wrong is an unlikely plan for success.

It is little wonder that so many people's perceptions of the economy are influenced by politicians—who can get reelected by playing to people's fears—rather then listening to experienced and proven economists like John. Most people know the size of the federal debt (because they've heard politicians complain about it) but have no idea about the size of our national income or assets. (Quick—do you?) Those numbers are every bit as important in understanding our economy as our federal debt.

In short, most people confuse the financial condition of the federal government with the financial condition of the country. They are related, but they are *not* identical. Look at it this way: if your business is strong and its value is growing, then it is unlikely that you will go bankrupt just because your checking account is running a small deficit. Yet, our national anxiety is such that we are so focused on the deficit in our checking account that we feel we need to completely overhaul our business to compensate. A different kind of transformation may be more appropriate.

THE TRUTH DEEP WITHIN

Liberals and conservatives want the quick fix. Rather than disciplining ourselves and our children, we ask others to make us stop before we sin again. It is easier to persuade ourselves that government should restore our lost virtue, rather than make the effort to live a virtuous life so that others might do likewise.

Cal Thomas

Not long ago I heard a talk by the president of a major conservative seminary who said that one of the first things he did upon becoming president of the seminary was to install a camera in the bookstore. Too many seminarians were neglecting to pay for their books and supplies. He felt the camera was largely responsible for increasing the revenue of the bookstore by $1,000,000 the following year. His second policy was to require seminarians to attend church on Sunday. Too many were using it to wash the car, sleep in, and so on.

A few days later, the *Wall Street Journal* ran a feature titled "Looking for God in All The Wrong Places," which quipped, "U.S. history is a battle between two conceptions of evil. In one, Satan is a dark force inside all of us. In the other, Satan steers other people but never oneself. Lately these two models have come close to beating each other to death, leaving us with no clear view of what evil means."[5]

Those are both sad but important commentaries on our time. As a conservative speaker, I always find it tempting, easy, and popular to point to the mischief caused by liberal lawmakers, bureaucrats, educators, and talk-show producers. I also find it more truthful, difficult, but enriching to look into my soul—and into the conservative mind in general. It is easy to hate "big government," "multinational corporations," or "foreigners"—even though they are actually our neighbors whom we have been commanded to love.

Many conservatives, I believe, hate government in general but love it in particular. We say we dislike big government, and yet we want it to insure our bank deposits and bonds against default; we want it to protect us from criminals by hiring more police and building more prisons; we want it to protect our industries from inexpensive imports by establishing tariffs and to protect our borders from inexpensive labor; and much more. I have grown increasingly concerned that many of my fellow conservatives simply think that they must convert Pharaoh to make their lives easier. But Moses never considered that an option. He never tried to conform the governing powers to his image. Rather, he led his people on a difficult and very personal journey across the desert sands to freedom. They willingly followed–until economic anxiety struck them in the desert. Then they wanted to return to Egypt "where at least we have bread." But Moses led on toward freedom.

John's approach to life is along this same difficult but enriching path. Personal discovery and self-sacrifice enlarge the soul. Self-interested politics does not. In the fifteen years that I have studied him from near and far, I have discovered something curious: neither I nor his closest associates know much, if anything, about his political views. He generally believes, of course, that limited government is a good thing and that private charity is preferable to government welfare. But about his political affiliations or preferences, we know very little. Therefore, the following political views are my own, not John's, but I thought you should know them since they influence my perspective on the economy and how you might successfully invest for the future.

For what it's worth, my academic degree is in political science. Like many baby boomers, I began to lose my faith in government during the late sixties as I pursued my degree, and what little faith I had left collapsed as the conservative "law-and-order" presidency of Richard Nixon collapsed.

Like the Israelites, I too began to wander the sands of truth; I too began to understand why Solomon said, "Put not your trust in human princes" (note that Solomon did not specify "liberal" or "conservative" princes).

Ultimately, my experience has led me to believe that moral problems have fewer political solutions than many of us believe. As a result, I also have fewer expectations of government than many people seem to. Oddly enough, I suppose that is why I am not particularly angry with our government—as politically incorrect as that may sound. Anger is a reaction to unfulfilled expectations, and since I have so few expectations of government, I am just not that angry with it.

Still, politics is somewhat important. Government, at its various levels, controls about one-third of the American economy through taxing and spending. It influences more through such programs as deposit insurance and tax breaks for retirement savings. It is difficult to discuss your economic future without delving into the subject of politics. So if I had to categorize my current political thinking—though I hope it transcends any categories generally recognized today—it would be similar to the neoconservative impulse: a blend of heart, soul, and mind.

My family has always been conservative. My father was the first person I can remember who said Social Security was a bad idea. I still have a card somewhere that says I'm a sustaining member of the Republican National Committee (while I wondered how it reflected the new austerity of Washington—the most recent was actually a "gold card"!). It has often been said that neoconservatives are liberals who were mugged by reality during the sixties, but my background indicates that neoconservatives can also be conservatives who were mugged by the realities of Vietnam, Watergate, the savings-and-loan mess, and the escapades of Wall Street during the eighties.

THE JOURNEY
Time and again, I hear the raised voices of our would-be prophets, claiming that the cause of all our troubles is "them." . . . What we really need

right now is a voice akin to the Hebrew prophets who will call us to look for the demonic within ourselves.

Tony Campolo

In short, each of us aspires to the same promised land as John Templeton. He simply knows a different way there and has a different perspective of the giants and riches that await us. Despite his great wealth, joy, and hope for the future, be assured that he knows life is a difficult journey, filled with many gains and losses. He almost surrendered his hard-won place at Yale University during the depths of the Depression due to lack of funds. He and his wife furnished their first home for $25 by buying second-hand furniture. They made a pact to save 50% of their income during their early years so they could spend their golden years achieving their fondest dreams. But in mid-life, he lost his wife in a tragic traffic accident. He recently lost his second wife after a lingering illness. He is surely personification of the words of the lyricist that soul is "about faith, a deeper devotion and a joy that comes out of sorrow."

In many ways, John's journey to success is simply an ongoing sequel to the ancient one. It is not of battles with the external giants of our time, as imagined by many, but of the struggles deep within the human heart, soul, and mind. As such, it could offer direction into the new millennium. And who knows? Should Americans grow weary enough of the age of anxiety to ask what is truly bothering us, John's belief that spiritual progress is always life's highest priority might help us to find peace. And that might once again fill our blessed land with the riches of hope and joy.

two

COUNT YOUR BLESSINGS

GOLDEN RULE:
Count your blessings to enrich yourself and your neighbors, first spiritually, and then, perhaps, financially

Do not be anxious about anything, but in everything, by prayer and petition, with thanksgiving, present your requests to God. And the peace of God, which transcends all understanding, will guard your hearts and your minds in Christ Jesus. Finally, brothers, whatever is true, whatever is noble, whatever is right, whatever is pure, whatever is lovely, whatever is admirable—if anything is excellent or praiseworthy—think about such things.

(Philippians 4:6–8)

LOUIS RUKEYSER: "Is something wrong with the American Spirit?"

SIR JOHN TEMPLETON: "Yes, yes, Louis—that is the right way to put it! America is still the land of opportunity, the land of entrepreneurship. But we are negative minded. It's a pity. The truth is far better than the mood of the American people. You can find plenty of things to worry about if you're determined to look for them. But if you look for the good things, they're far more numerous than the bad."

*I*f asked to name the single most important economic lesson I have learned from Sir John Templeton, I would probably quote something he told me a few years back: "The wealth of a nation does not depend on natural resources. It depends on what goes on in the hearts and minds of its people."

31

Think about this: for thousands of years oil lay beneath the sands of the Middle East, but it was of no use to anyone. Then, when someone thought of turning it into usable energy, it became a valuable form of wealth. How we think about the things around us is terribly important. It can determine our success. And I believe many of us are not thinking in ways that lead to success.

A few years ago, I met with John and Mark Holowesko, who was chosen to assume the management responsibilities of the largest Templeton funds after John retired in 1992. In that meeting, Holowesko said, "America doesn't have a clue as to how competitive it is on the world scene," and he told this story. As he was flying out of New York the previous day, he noticed below him someone on a very large tractor pulling a wide mowing machine beside the interstate. An hour later he arrived at the Nassau airport and drove to the Templeton headquarters. As he drove, he noticed ten men cutting grass alongside one of the major roads—a road that would not be considered a major thoroughfare in the U.S. Each man was using a hand-held sickle.

One American with a tractor, he observed, was probably a hundred times more productive cutting grass than ten Bahamians. (Economists call this the "comparative advantage" that technology bestows on industrialized nations.) Yet many Americans feel threatened by the fact the Bahamians are "low-cost, Third World labor," making one-tenth of what the American was probably making.

The *Wall Street Journal* agrees that we worry too much about our poor neighbors:

> It's easy to cite big U.S. companies that fired workers at home and set up shop overseas. But trade isn't big enough to depress wages all across the $7 trillion U.S. economy. Since 1970, manufactured imports from developing countries have surged, but by 1994 still equaled only 3.5% of the overall economy. Most service jobs—clerks, technicians, consultants—aren't affected at all by trade.[1]

Of course, some Americans believe that nine other American workers are out of jobs because of the productivity of that one fellow on the tractor, but such people simply haven't grasped the fact that those workers are employed in modern factories making tractors and mowing machines, rather than cutting grass in the hot sun. Others, in the service sector of our economy, repair and maintain those tractors and mowing machines. Even more people, in the information sector, think of increasingly better ways to build and service them. All in all, our economy has generated 60 million new jobs since 1960. According to the *Economist*, the U.S. has generated 38 million net new jobs in the past twenty years alone, while Western Europe created *no* net new jobs.

Yet I like Holowesko's story because it rings true. I grew up in a poor rural area of Kentucky where I spent endless summer days mowing grass. My father eventually purchased a John Deere dealership, which helped put me through the university, so that now I help others understand how to own shares of companies like John Deere. In essence, despite the great economic changes in my lifetime (I even work at a profession that did not exist when I was born), I am not anxious. I'm grateful I no longer mow grass in the hot sun, especially at the wages my father paid his young son.

AMERICA'S WEALTH

When I was born, the uniform wage of an unskilled man was only ten cents an hour. Now the average American factory worker earns over one hundred times that. Even after adjusting for inflation, the increase is still more than eleven fold. . . . If you look further back to 1776, you will see that 85% of the world's population had to work in agriculture just to produce enough food. Today less than 4% work on farms in America and they produce great surpluses.

Sir John M. Templeton

The American economy will produce more than $7 trillion worth of goods and services this year. In spite of the fact that, according to surveys, a large percentage of Americans believe the Japanese economy is even larger, Japan actually produces only about $2.5 trillion—less than 40% of ours.

The average American paycheck buys about $25,000 worth of goods and services each year. That's over 15% more than the typical Japanese paycheck, which buys about $21,000 worth.

Since our recession ended in the early 1990s, and the Japanese bubble began to leak air at the same time, the numbers have grown even further apart, even more quickly. But unlike the trends of the 1980s, which favored the Japanese, the more recent numbers are rarely mentioned in the popular media. They should be. Our economy is far from perfect, but its ability to produce jobs, goods, and services is unparalleled in human history—and many Americans are being enriched.

An article in the December 1995 edition of the *Reader's Digest* posed this question: "Where's the middle class going?" And it gave an unusual answer. It said that since the sixties, the number of American families earning an inflation-adjusted equivalent of $100,000 a year has risen from just over 1,000,000 to about 6,000,000 today. I doubt that could be said for any other nation on earth.

It is hard to imagine, but statistics tell us that only 10% of Americans had televisions when I was born in 1950. More than a third of our homes lacked indoor plumbing. A similar percentage did not have telephones. Air-conditioning was rare. An estimated one-third of all Americans lived in poverty.

Looking back even further, life expectancy was only forty years when Lincoln was president. It is over seventy-five years today, largely because we no longer have to work ourselves to death, as many used to. The *Economist* has noted, "In 1881, a typical male manual worker clocked up an estimated 154,000 hours over his lifetime. Today, thanks to longer periods of education, shorter working weeks, longer holidays and earlier retirement, 65,000 hours might be typical in a rich industrial country."[2]

In short, despite the distractions that keep us from this truth, America has been blessed with both great wealth and the freedom to use it. But how come we seldom hear about it?

Several years ago, the conservative Heritage Foundation published an *Index of Leading Cultural Indicators*, which portrayed America as experiencing a serious cultural decline. This publication was widely quoted and discussed, no doubt because of its negative stance and bleak conclusions. Then, later, the foundation published an *Index of Economic Freedoms*, which compared the wealth of over a hundred nations with their taxes, regulations, property rights, and other measures of economic freedom. The United States was rated the freest and, by far, the richest major nation on earth. In contrast to the earlier study, this more encouraging report was not mentioned in the popular media except on the editorial page of the *Wall Street Journal*.[3]

More recently, the *Economist* commissioned a panel of world-class economists, like Milton Friedman, to study the economic freedoms enjoyed by twenty major nations. The panel ranked the United States second, just behind New Zealand.[4] Again, the good news did not exactly resound throughout the land.

It is important for us to understand this positive aspect of the U.S. economy. People constantly tell me they are vaguely anxious about the economy, but when pressed, they can't cite a single statistic to justify their concern. Knowing the facts about our economy and how it relates to our world can make a big difference in how you feel about your future. I know from personal experience.

A few years ago, I was invited to speak at a symposium in Uganda, a lovely country that Winston Churchill once described as "the pearl of Africa"—that is, before dictator Idi Amin crushed its economy and murdered tens of thousands of its citizens. Nevertheless, the survivors of Amin's reign were beginning to discuss ways of rebuilding their nation. They began by converting their socialistic economy to a market economy, planning their first stock exchange, and laying the groundwork for a constitutional convention. At that point, the Church of England and the Archbishop of Uganda thought it might be timely to organize a symposium of business, political, and religious leaders. So it was that I was invited to speak about the moral foundations of political economy and personal financial management.

As I researched my presentation, I discovered that the typical Ugandan paycheck buys about $200 worth of goods and services—each year. That is less than 1% of our purchasing power. It is about what I spend on Diet Pepsi in a year's time—and yet, it is fairly typical of about one-fifth of the world's population, or about one billion people.

We had been at the international conference center in Kampala for about a week when my wife, Sherry, and I began to discuss our new Ugandan friends. I remarked that they seemed intelligent, well-educated, and deeply religious. But they seemed to possess one trait that we would all like to have. They seemed to live without the anxiety that we Americans take for granted.

That journey changed my life, for it taught me how to count the blessings of living in America. A year after we returned, I rarely complained about our political economy and how it might be better. That trip freed me to be a more confident investor, a more generous giver to charitable causes, and someone who takes the time to do the meaningful things he loves to do. In short, if someone were to ask me now what it would take to make my dreams come true, I would reply, "What I have right now."

The Elusive American Dream

"Each year the Roper Organization conducts a survey asking Americans how much annual income they would need to fulfill their dreams. This year's average response was $102,000. In 1992, the figure was $83,000.

"We wanted to know more—not just about the price people put on happiness but also about what happiness means to them. We dispatched more than a dozen writers and photographers across the country to talk to people. Several clear patterns did emerge from the responses.

"One is that the more money people have, the more they believe they need. Another pattern: The less money people have, the more likely they are to think of others as they articulate their dreams. The well-heeled immediately rattled off a list of things they wanted for themselves. The less well-off cited things they wanted for their loved ones—to help a brother get out of debt, to help a wife get an education. One man said he'd like to buy pickup trucks for his grandchildren.

"What does this tell us? Perhaps self-centeredness is part of what it takes to get rich in this country. Perhaps success itself breeds greed. Or maybe the well-off spend too much of their time associating with other people who are well-off—and lose touch with the many folks they could conceivably help."

Worth magazine (January 1996)

Because of my experience in Africa, I can echo the sentiments of author Tim Stafford, who wrote about his recent visit to neighboring Kenya:

I have had to question, though, why the faculty of hope seems so little present in American public life today. It was disorienting to leave Africa and return to America where people seem relentlessly bitter and complaining about a government that would be the dream of any African, about an economy that would be the dream of any African, about a justice system that would be the dream of any African, about a medical system that would be the dream of any African.... It is not merely that we have leisure time to think and formulate complaints; the Africans I talked to are educated men and women who have time, too. But they have a different spirit.[5]

My years of investment counseling indicate that our low spirits may be the result of our high expectations. I'm always amazed how a company's stock tends to drop sharply after the company announces that its quarterly earnings are 20% above those of last year—all because the analysts are unhappy because they had been *expecting* a 30% increase.

This pattern holds true for politics and economics as well as stocks. Our Founding Fathers wrote in the Constitution that our government should *promote* the general welfare, but we now *expect* it to provide for our personal welfare as well. The Founding Fathers saw the wisdom in making changes thoughtfully and gradually, so they instituted a system of checks and balances that made it more difficult for individual human passions to do general harm. But now we *expect* a revolution after each election and our spirits sink when changes are small and slow.

Economically, we used to pray for our daily bread, but we now *expect* our companies to provide cafeteria-style benefit programs. As investors, we used to hope for a reasonable return on our money. Will Rogers even said he just hoped for the return of his money! Today, we *expect* high returns the likes of which John Templeton never achieved in his remarkable career.

Since grandiose expectations have the potential of threatening our financial success—as they most definitely threaten our spiritual success—it's worth exploring their origins.

THE ROOT OF AMERICAN ANXIETY

It is a delightful and profitable occupation to mark the hand of God in the lives of ancient saints, and to observe His goodness in delivering them, His mercy in pardoning them, and His faithfulness in keeping His covenant with them. But would it not be even more interesting and profitable for us to notice the hand of God in our own lives?

Charles H. Spurgeon

In ancient times, the Greek philosopher Plato compared life to a cave in which we sit in semi-darkness and watch shadows on the walls. We grow to believe those shadows are reality, not merely the diversions from the greater reality outside the cave. Occasionally, a great teacher enters the cave to enlighten us about a brighter world outside, but because we prefer our shadowy illusions to enlightened reality, these remarkable teachers are rejected, scorned, or even made to suffer martyrdom.

This same principle is at work in the case of personal financial management. It is easier to avoid the reality of our national wealth than to live with the responsibility of it—and yet, we need to assume this responsibility on a very personal level if our country is ever to reclaim a feeling of its own greatness. As Churchill said, "The price of greatness is responsibility."

So how do we identify the shadows that delay our journey out of the cave and into the greater success that our Good Teacher, Jesus, wants for us? First, in this Information Age of five hundred television channels, talk radio, and financial magazines and newsletters, two shadows are increasingly problematic: the popular media and politicians. Either can encourage pessimism. But if your economic perspective is shaped by any popular medium that is politically influenced, your world-view is probably somewhere between pessimism and paranoia. But I have good news for you: true economists rarely agree with the economic opinions of the media pundits and the politicians.

THE POPULAR MEDIA

What lies behind us and what lies before us are small matters compared to what lies within us.

Ralph Waldo Emerson

How do you start your day? If you are like I used to be, you pour a cup of coffee, open the newspaper, and turn on a morning television news show, which, with a jolt, presents you with an endless file of politicians and reporters telling how wrong everything is with your world, and countless advertisers telling you how wrong everything is with your lifestyle.

John Templeton recommends a different approach. Lie silently in bed when you first awaken and think of five new ways you have been blessed. Try it for a few weeks. I think you'll find it enriching, and peace will take root in your life.

John, who has had both good and bad encounters with the media over the years, once told me in an interview:

> There has always been something in human nature that makes you buy a newspaper that has the most horrible headline. Because of that, to be successful in the publishing or television business, you have to feed the public these catastrophes or the negative viewpoint. Therefore, the public is brainwashed. There are not enough people

who are independent enough to do their own analysis and studying and see that, yes, there are problems but for every problem there are at least ten blessings."

In 1992, he told the Templeton share holders that this may only be a successful strategy for the media in the short-run:

It's very interesting to me that the spread of communications has increased the misery of people . . . we're flooded with bad news. And this bad news is making people depressed at a time when prosperity is at its greatest ever. And I notice it particularly when reading the newspapers. The newspapers will interpret almost anything in bearish terms. And this has a depressing effect. I believe, though that it will wear off. I believe that there's only a certain amount of bad news that we can take. As we get used it, we will gradually learn to overlook it—just as the people in the communist nations began to overlook what was in their newspapers. It had been wrong for so long that they just ignored it. And I believe that we'll learn to ignore the pessimism in our media.

Economist Louis Rukeyser agrees:

Ever since we were first warned about crossing the street alone, we've been conditioned to think of grim warnings as stark reality. On the other hand, we're also trained to be wary of purveyors of sunshine and bliss. Optimists, we feel, may turn out to be three bricks shy of a load. That's why we barely hear bullish forecasts—while whispers of impending doom shake our souls. It's also why your mailbox is stuffed with pitches that herald each market downtick as the first raindrop of a flood that will wipe out life as we know it. No doubt about it, pessimism pays. Unfortunately, it pays mostly to those who dispense it.[6]

Whatever you think of the irrepressible Rush Limbaugh, it's worth paying attention to something he recently said:

The prosperity currently enjoyed by ordinary U.S. citizens is unprecedented in human history. Yet in the aggregate, the information coming from the dominant media conveys exactly the opposite impression. . . . Bad economic news is reported often, prominently and at length, while good economic news is down-played or omitted. As a result, many Americans are completely uninformed about the economic standing of the U.S. vis-à-vis the rest of the world. . . . The American press has done this country an enormous disservice. We have been treated to story after story of America in decline. The reports of a faltering U.S. have become so pervasive that a huge proportion of American citizens believe them and make crucial political and economic decisions on the basis of these stories. The sad image of a once-great but now crumbling country, a pitiful giant, is a commonplace perception. It is also a lie.[7]

Limbaugh went on to quote studies that said 85% of the economic news from the popular media during the past decade has been negative. Yet I believe the more important part of his analysis is the statement, "good economic news is down-played or omitted." Keep in mind that the Dow Jones Average actually rose 500% during the time studied—as worries about high interest rates, oil shortages, Japan, and communism appeared and disappeared from our front pages.

John Paulos, a professor of mathematics, has written the book *A Mathematician Reads the Newspaper*. He speaks of the "use, misuse, and neglect of numbers" in the news and concludes that we need to be very careful about how statistics are presented by the media. He likes to illustrate the problem by using the earth's population as an example. A pessimist, Paulos notes, might tell us that if all the people in the world were stacked end to end, we could reach to the moon and back eight times. That sounds pretty crowded! But an optimist might say that all the people in the world could fit in the Grand Canyon and each person would still have a cube of space twenty feet on each side (that's eight thousand cubic feet). That is just as correct but sounds less threatening.

Again, the same principle applies to economics. Take, for example, our federal debt. It is about $5 trillion. One pessimistic political organization exclaimed, "The federal debt would produce a stack of $1,000 bills over 300 miles into space!" which is true. But have you ever heard the value of our nation's assets? It would amount to a stack of $1,000 bills that would reach about 3,000 miles into space. That economic fact sounds a little more encouraging, doesn't it? And have you ever thought an optimist can talk about "wage stability" and a pessimist can talk about "wage stagnation" and be talking about the same numbers!

A more balanced perspective about our economy can have tremendous ramifications for your financial and spiritual success—though it may have even larger ramifications for our nation. In fact, our Founding Fathers thought democracy could only succeed when the electorate was informed enough to support our leaders in making important decisions.

So it's troubling when the *Washington Post* reports that "a major new test has revealed that most Americans are abysmally ignorant of basic economic and financial facts of life." The professor who conducted the test for Merrill Lynch commented, "Most Americans simply don't possess an understanding of even the most basic financial and economic concepts." He noted that two-thirds of the survey's respondents would not even hazard a guess as to the level of the Dow Jones Industrial Average and only 14% knew the general range. Only one-third knew who the head of the Federal Reserve Board was. When asked about the size of the annual federal budget deficit, only 11% could come within $150 billion of it. (I found that especially interesting since virtually everyone I know worries about it so much.) Only 13% knew the highest Social Security benefit for a two-person household was between $15,000 and $30,000, a pretty broad range. Yet a higher percentage of Americans feel that UFOs exist than feel they will receive Social Security benefits in the future. Eight reporters took the test and three failed.

Daniel P. Tully, the chairman of Merrill Lynch, commented: "The results are shockingly low. We believe that this test goes to the heart of a very important issue, the ability of Americans to manage the economic decisions they must make day-to-day in order to prepare effectively for the future."[8]

While the clients I deal with daily are anything but dumb, they are often ignorant of their blessings and are often confused about the true state of the economy. And no wonder. Neither the liberal secular media nor the conservative Christian media has been sharing the full story.

SLEEPING AT NIGHT

The level of pessimism in America is just not proportional to the problems that America has. During the presidential election, Americans were told they ranked thirteenth in the world in terms of income. That's so far from the truth I couldn't believe that was being told to people. Who cares if the average salary in Switzerland is $20,000 versus $16,000 in America when it takes four times as much to live in Switzerland? When you adjust for purchasing power parity, Americans absolutely have the highest standard of living in the world.

Mark Holowesko, *Equities* magazine (December 1992)

A friend of my wife's—I'll call her Mary—is a troubling example of how both the secular and religious media can team with politics to prove "a little knowledge is a dangerous thing," especially to our spiritual well-being. Her story is also important from a financial standpoint, since it is doubtful that anyone can be a productive member of a family—or a society—if he or she can't sleep at night.

Mary and her husband, Tom, once joined my wife, Sherry, and me for breakfast at a time when the Federal Reserve Board had just raised interest rates several times in an attempt to cool an economy that was growing too quickly. Mary said she had not been sleeping. When Sherry asked why, Mary replied, "I'm worried about the economy." She said she had been reading troubling things about the economy in the papers; hearing troubling things about the federal debt from Rush Limbaugh; and seeing troubling things about both when watching the evening news. She then added that when she turned on her favorite conservative televangelist and Christian financial talk-show host, they said the same things—"So it must be true."

I wish Mary had read a book by Bruce Howard, a professor of economics at Wheaton College, called *Safe and Sound: The Strength and Stability of the U.S. Economy*. It demonstrates how much of what we believe to be true about our economy is political illusion painted by our liberal and conservative friends in the media. Howard concludes, "Christians should spend less time worrying about the remote chance of needing to survive economic calamity and get back to thinking about more important issues of the kingdom."

On a personal level, Mary's fear is intriguing because her husband, Tom, owns a successful business that about 99% of the world's people would love to call their own. He employs a couple dozen people. They live in an affluent community. Tom plays golf twice a week, and they enjoy nice vacations. Mary also has the financial freedom to stay home with her children each day.

Her fear is also interesting politically, for in all the years I have known her, I have never heard Mary express a political thought. Yet with a little encouragement, she eventually identified her anxiety as being rooted in the perception that our federal debt and government spending are out of control. Still, she seemed totally unaware that virtually all of Tom's business came from government contracts. In other words, her children's daily bread, and quite possibly their futures, are directly related to what many of the conservative politicians she votes for might consider government waste, though Tom was quick to point out how many jobs and benefits were provided by his private company.

With a little soul-searching, we might acknowledge that, at the very least, we conservatives acquiesce to political anger, even when it threatens our spiritual progress. Heather Higgins, who co-hosts a television show with Speaker of the House Newt Gingrich, recently told an interviewer for *Religion and Liberty* that before the 1994 election she knew "people who were angry and upset would have a much higher motivation to vote." But deliberately sowing pessimism and anger among the electorate by "going negative" can produce a bitter crop of citizens once we are asked to govern.

For these reasons, all of us should think twice as we listen to talk radio. The conservative think-tank Empower America recently interviewed Michael Harrison, the editor and publisher of *Talkers* magazine, the major trade publication for the talk-radio industry. Empower America asked him, "Do you consider talk radio to have more entertainment value, news, or education value?"

Mr. Harrison replied:

> Ah, now that's the question talk radio programmers are constantly wrestling with. Finding the perfect balance between information and entertainment. This is not a media characteristic peculiar to talk radio. Television news, newspapers, even presidential campaigns are preoccupied with capturing attention and developing interest. Or to put it another way, to avoid being boring at all costs— even if it means *leaving out important information or glossing over serious, complex issues*. [Emphasis mine.][9]

The media's ability to shape Mary's anxious worldview is probably most intriguing from a theological perspective. Tom and Mary are Roman Catholics, but Mary's perspective of our political economy seems far more influenced by the secular media and the Religious Right than by the Catholic Church. Pope John Paul, who is a profound political and economic thinker has said,

> We must not be afraid of the future. We must not be afraid of man. We have within us the capacities for wisdom and virtue. With these gifts, and with the help of God's grace, we can build in the next century and the next millennium a civilization worthy of the human person, a true culture of freedom. We can and must do so! And in doing

so, we shall see that the tears of this century have prepared the ground for a new springtime of the human spirit.

Yet his message of well-being hadn't reached my friends. And I find the same sense of hope is often missing among Baptists and mainline church members as well.

One of the reasons for this phenonmenon may be that many church leaders have lost hope and are increasingly anxious themselves. You probably haven't thought about it, but many of my friends in the denominations feel they are in an "industry" that is downsizing very rapidly. And they are most anxious that their education and skills aren't greatly marketable in the "post-Christian culture" that America has become. You could perform a wonderful ministry to them by explaining that, if we get our own act together, the baby boomers are on the verge of making religion a "growth industry" again. The clergy might then become what our friend Henri Nouwen calls "wounded healers," equipped with the difficult experiences to help all of us deal with the anxieties of a world where creativity is increasing at ever greater rates. Then, there will be no shortage of demand for their skills in the future.

The church, both Catholic and Protestant, could fill a tremendous void in American life if it intelligently shared *all* the information needed to achieve spiritual and financial success. That may even be the key to the church becoming relevant to our culture again. It may also be the key to greater funding for our churches, ministries, and charities. It has been said that anxiety is love's greatest killer. If anxiety about the future keeps people from investing in it, it will also prevent them from giving for it—and there is evidence that this has been happening.

Every two years, Independent Sector, a group dedicated to the study and development of charitable giving, conducts the most comprehensive survey of giving in the U.S. Since 1990 it has been saying that economic pessimism is a major reason Americans aren't giving as much as we used to. (Pessimists give about 50% less than optimists of comparable income.) Reporting on the 1994 study, the *Wall Street Journal* said,

> Despite an improved economy and stepped-up volunteer programs, Americans worried more about their financial future and donated less of their time and money over recent years. President of Independent Sector, Sara Melendez, said, "Americans seem to be more insecure about their economic futures. I guess it hasn't come home to everyone that the economy is getting better." Vice president

Virginia Hodgkinson added, "As soon as people feel confident that this economy is strong and will last, giving will pick up."[10]

So it is in the interests of churches and charities for us to count our blessings and help our people discern economic reality from political illusion.

POLITICAL ILLUSION

Politicians earn much of their living by exploiting anxieties, encouraging people to feel worse than they should about the state of their country.
                                                          The Economist

Not long after the new 1993 tax laws were enacted, several of my clients called me. They were nervous because one man, who also happened to be a friend of mine, had said on a nationally syndicated conservative talk show that the new laws were "the largest tax increase in history." Best described as an ultraconservative, my friend regularly beats his drum to the steady rhythm that America's economy is doomed because it is overtaxed and suffering from socialistic strangulation.

So it didn't surprise me that he never mentioned such quotes from the *Economist* as, "Bureaucrats and their 'waste, fraud and abuse' make good whipping boys; but they account for only a few billion dollars of the deficit." Or "Nobody could pretend that America's tax system is perfect. Its faults do not, however, lie in the overall level of taxation—by international standards, America remains a lightly taxed country."[11]

It would undoubtedly surprise the talk show's listeners that as Congress was still debating the budget in late 1995, the November 13 edition of the *Wall Street Journal* shared the news that the federal government's tax "share of GDP [gross domestic product] has stayed remarkably near 19% for twenty years now." Jack Kemp made the same point as he announced the findings of his flat-tax commission.

Nor did it surprise me that my friend didn't share the good news that virtually every serious economic publication—notice I didn't say political publication—says federal spending as a percentage of our economy peaked at 25% in 1984 and has declined to about 21% today, almost exactly where it was both in 1980 and forty years ago. (Note: the difference between 19% taxes and the 21% spending is the deficit.)

Clearly, most of this is due to the strength of the economy, not the strength of our political process, so it surprised me when my friend went on to say that the tax act would eventually destroy the economy. He even counseled listeners to sell all their stocks and move the proceeds to government bonds. I was amused that my friend who spoke so negatively about financing the government through paying taxes would want to finance it through buying government bonds! It made me wonder if he was philosophically opposed to government or simply opposed to the idea of paying it money rather than it paying him money.

Yet the most important lesson from this bit of human folly is summed up in a line from the Bible: "As a man thinks, so he is." During almost twenty years of investment counseling, I have found little wisdom more useful.

In the 1970s, many people I counseled thought there was little need to save and invest because, they thought, the government would care for them. So they didn't save or invest. In the early 1980s, many people devoted their time and money to pursuing even more money, and they usually became more prosperous but not happier. In the late 1980s, I began to work with clients who thought they should devote their time and money to pursuing both financial and spiritual wealth—and they usually became more prosperous and happier people.

During the 1990s, however, I have tried—and failed—to help people who are convinced that they can't prosper or be happy due to our government. So while I make a good moral, economic, and spiritual case for less government interference in our lives, I won't let political illusion keep you or me from making the crucial investments we need to make for future success.

BANKING ON POLITICIANS

Politicians are lousy investment advisors.
David Goldman, Managing Director, Bear, Stearns & Co.

As the political rhetoric about taxes peaked in 1993, John Templeton told us he owned no bonds—because he believed the economy was strengthening rapidly, which would make interest rates rise, and, in turn, hurt bond prices. As he told *The Wall Street Journal* at the time, "The risk in cash and bonds is greater than usual—and the risk in stocks is not."[12]

So while I favor limited taxes and regulation, I shared with my clients this perspective offered by the *Economist* on August 7, 1993, only a few days after John recommended that investors stick with stocks: "Mr. Dole, like other Republicans, has tried to scare Americans into believing that the tax increases are aimed at the middle classes, which they are not. . . . Two-thirds of Americans have swallowed the Republican line and believe, wrongly, that Mr. Clinton has put up middle-class taxes substantially."

The *Wall Street Journal* threw additional light on things later when it said,

> Much of the GOP's budget-bashing shows how aggressive cam-
> paigning can stretch the facts. Contrary to Republican claims, the
> 1993 package with a $240 billion tax increase is not "the largest tax
> increase in history." The 1982 deficit-reduction package of President
> Reagan and Sen. Robert Dole in a GOP-controlled Senate was a big-
> ger tax bill, both in 1993-adjusted dollars and as a percentage of the
> overall economy; and both recent laws are dwarfed by the tax bills of
> World War II.[13]

Unfortunately, many of my clients thought that political illusions were only created by the other party, so they followed my friend's advice and moved from stocks to bonds. Of course, just as John predicted, 1994 was the worst year for bonds since the Great Depression, and the stock market soared in 1995.

My intent is not to cast aspersions on Republicans; Democrats have their share of political illusions as well. You should remember that President Clinton's campaign themes were "The Economy, Stupid" and the need for change—even as John was investing billions of dollars into shares of U.S. companies. The president, no doubt, will brag about the economy and resist change as the campaign of 1996 progresses, so I still find it enriching to negotiate the political thicket with more objectivity.

Remember, *no* opposition party is going to echo the town crier and say that, at this hour when the land is governed by the other party, all is well. To regain power, the opposition cry must inevitably be that radical change is needed. Unfortunately, Republicans were the opposition party going into the elections of 1994 and 1996.

In short, few of us can afford political illusions—and there will always be an opposition party around. So I suggest you build your financial and spiritual well-being on foundations of economic reality. I deeply believe this approach will help our nation sleep better at night and be more productive the next day.

ECONOMIC REALITY

When the basic direction of reality changes, you've got to get with it.
David Stockman, President Reagan's Budget Director

Not long ago, a prominent politician from Georgia said:

> Our government in Washington now is a horrible bureaucratic mess. It is disorganized, wasteful, has no purpose, and its policies— when they exist—are incomprehensible or devised by special-interest groups with little or no regard for the welfare of the average American citizen. . . . We've developed in recent years a welfare government. We've seen evolve a bloated, confused, bureaucratic mess. The American people believe that we ought to control our government. On the other hand, we've seen our government more and more controlling us.[14]

Can you guess who said that? It sounds like something Newt Gingrich would say in 1996, doesn't it? But it wasn't. It was Jimmy Carter speaking in 1976. My point is this: inefficiency in government may simply be one of those unpleasant realities of life—one that hasn't changed much since Jesus spoke of "rendering unto Caesar."

But that doesn't mean that economic reality can't change. In the August 16, 1990, edition of *Outstanding Investor Digest*, long before the political revolution of 1994, John shared his perspective that our economic reality was quite possibly taking a turn for the better:

> I would say that this is one of the great turning points in world history. The conquest of England in 1066 and the discovery of the Americas in 1492 were great turning points. The Industrial Revolution was a great turning point. And our children and grandchildren will learn that 1989 was a great turning point in world history— toward greater freedom, greater prosperity, greater brotherhood and toward increased religion. So that we are standing today at a historic time—at a time that does offer some opportunities to investors.

There's an old saying that perception lags behind reality. As I have counseled investors during the first half of this decade, I've found that relatively few have caught up with the economic reality John saw back then. There's no better way to take a giant step toward that reality, and toward success, than by exploring the political illusion that has cost more investors more spiritual peace and financial opportunities during the past decade than any other—debt, especially our federal debt.

three

THE NATIONAL
DEBT AND YOUR FUTURE

> ## GOLDEN RULE:
> *Debt, whether personal or collective,*
> *should not keep you from investing in your future*

"Whoever watches the wind will not plant; whoever looks at the clouds will not reap."

(Ecclesiastes 11:4)

I am tired of hearing our politicians, liberal and conservative, pontificate on "the American Dream"—how we are falling short of it, frustrating it, neglecting it, and in general allowing ourselves to be cheated of it. Is that the way adults are supposed to talk? After all, the U.S. is just chock full of people—most of us, in fact—who have failed to realize our childish or youthful dreams. Fortunately, only a tiny minority of perpetual malcontents dwell endlessly on this normal human experience.

Objectionable as all this is on the personal level, it is far more problematic on the political level. Rhetoric about "the American Dream" is always bound to suggest that our current condition—economic, social, political—is flawed in some fundamental way, and that radical corrective action is absolutely needed. Though most Americans do not believe they live in a fundamentally flawed society, our politicians and our media have taken upon themselves the task of persuading the people that they do. Thus do unprincipled political ambition and unprincipled moral arrogance combine to import a destructive element into American life.

Irving Kristol, *The Wall Street Journal*

One day in 1995, Alan Greenspan, chairman of the Federal Reserve Board, spoke about his view of the economy. Reading the accounts later, however, it was extremely difficult to figure out exactly what he had said. *Liberty* magazine noted the following four headlines from four different newspaper accounts of Greenspan's talk:

"Greenspan Sees Chance of Recession" (*New York Times*)

"Recession Is Unlikely, Greenspan Concludes" (*Washington Post*)

"Recession Risk Up, Greenspan Says" (*Baltimore Sun*)

"Fed Chairman Doesn't See Recession on the Horizon" (*Wall Street Journal*)

Chairman Greenspan must have chuckled at those headlines. Actually, if he had seen a recession on the horizon, the last thing he would have done is to spread it across the front pages of our leading newspapers. Fortunately, most serious investors know to take the economic pronouncements of government leaders—and the media—with a large grain of salt, which is why the stock market doesn't rise or fall a couple hundred points every time such headlines appear. Unfortunately, most typical Americans don't know that. But they should.

Among Sir John Templeton's personal files, there is a copy of his February 9, 1984, speech to the Templeton shareholders. Despite the fact that stocks have risen over 400% since that day, his remarks may be even more pertinent today.

There are many things to worry about; and I don't know the solution to these great worries. But I do not think there are any more things to worry about now than there were at any other time I can remember. Every year going back to the time that I first began to study stocks, there have always been enormous things to worry about. No one knows how these things will be solved; but as of today, I believe the United States, the world, and the New York stock market have less to worry about than any time I can remember. Here are some of the things that we are worried about today.

One is the national deficit. The national deficit is very large, over $200 billion. That is a terrible thing, and it is worth learning about. It is hard to see how it is going to be solved. But let's look at it in proportion.

I don't believe that any deficit is good. In fact, I don't believe that any of us should borrow money. I believe it is basically wrong to borrow for consumption purposes. I believe it is wrong for any nation to borrow. Perhaps in business it is all right to borrow for business purposes to a limited extent.

Only once in my life did I ever borrow anything. I borrowed $10,000 at one time when I already had assets that I could count on and $50,000 saved up so I was not taking too much risk, and I borrowed only for a few months. Other than that I never borrowed anything.

I'm old enough to say that when I was young, if you had a mortgage on your house you did not tell anybody. And very few people had charge accounts and nobody had a credit card. It was unknown to buy an automobile without paying cash for it. Now I think those were the right ideas. Because we have gotten away from those not only in our family life but also in our national life, we are getting into trouble and we are having these enormous deficits.

I don't think we're going to pay off the debt. I would challenge you to think of more than two or three nations who ever paid off their debt. So what we are witnessing is a serious matter. But the deficits in the United States, as big as they are, in relation to the gross national product, are only one-half as great as Japan, roughly one-half as great as Canada, and so forth. So the size of our deficit is not disastrous. And I don't think it is going to be eliminated. I don't think there is going to be any end to it.

Now what will that mean? It will not mean what you see happening in the stock market now. The newspaper this morning said because we are going to have this big deficit, share prices are going down. And lots of other good economists are saying the same thing, because we can't seem to solve the deficit problem, share prices will go down. [Yet] government deficit has never caused deflation. It causes inflation. And inflation in the long run causes higher share prices.

If you look at what happens when nations have deficits, it means more business, more profits. If you wanted to have lower common stock prices or a deflation, you balance the budget. If Congress next month passed a law to balance the budget, there would be that much less money to spend and therefore you would normally expect deflation and lower prices, including common stock prices. The fact we have this enormous deficit is a reason to buy stocks, not sell them.

Notice something carefully: Templeton said that over a *decade* ago—when deficits were even higher than they are today. First, he believed, and still believes, that balanced budgets are desirable, but despite his ideals about how the world might be, he based his financial decisions on economic reality, while he continued to live his personal life according to his ideals. There is a moral in that. As the Serenity Prayer says, "We must change what we can, accept what we can't, and have the wisdom to know the difference."

Second, notice that he said the short-term economic impact of budget deficits is often the exact *opposite* of what the popular media tell us. When he gave this speech, the newspapers were reporting that the stock market would fall because of the deficits. More recently, they have been saying it might rise if the government were to balance its budget.

But the *Economist* questioned these assumptions:

> Government spending has already been falling steadily since 1991, taking some of the impetus out of the economy. But the Republicans' current budget-balancing schemes could ground it altogether. . . . The plans currently on the table, if enacted, would shave economic growth by about 0.3 percentage points a year through 2002. There are two good reasons, however, to discount this worry. First, many Republicans are not in any hurry to start cutting.[1]

My guess, by the way, is that we'll soon be hearing from the "growth" wing of the Republican Party, which is that faction less focused on reducing the mortgage on our home and more concerned with growing our businesses so we can pay our mortgage. This is already finding expression in the "flat-tax" movement, which will now be difficult to sell to our fellow Republicans because they have been taught in recent years that deficits are evil.

In any case, one of the reasons the *Economist* expressed concern may have been its understanding of economic history. In the Summer 1995 issue of *Public Policy* magazine, Frederick Thayer examined six previous periods in American history when the federal debt became politically incorrect and our politicians embarked on serious efforts to pay it off. Thayer detailed that depressions followed each effort.

Having said that, it's important to point out that simply eliminating our annual *deficit* is a modest effort compared to paying off our *accumulated debt*. Few reasonable politicians advocate paying the debt off— at least yet. But Thayer's look at economic history suggests that John's caution about slower business, and lower stock prices, is worth heeding if politicians don't start heeding economists.

Most of us aren't aware of it, but both the *Wall Street Journal* and the *Economist* editorialized *against* the balanced-budget amendment. The *Wall Street Journal* said:

> We've always had our doubts about the budget amendment idea. While politically appealing, it makes no particular sense economically.... To understand the economics, start here: If all American households were required to balance their budgets, no one could ever buy a house. Of course, households don't think about their budgets that way; they figure "balance" means meeting their mortgage payments.... Perhaps in their current euphoria Republicans feel confident about this question, but our advice is that they should look before they leap.[2]

And the *Economist* said:

> That many Americans have long favored amending the Constitution to forbid budget deficits is entirely understandable. The perpetual phony crisis of American fiscal policy has become dull beyond words: it is about time that the entire subject was simply legislated out of existence. Unfortunately, as 1995 may prove, attempts to do this are likely to go wrong. Worse, they may even cause real harm.[3]

Now reflect on this a moment. Most of the world's leading economic thinkers advocate balanced budgets but understand that the balanced-budget *amendment* is more of a convenient political tool than a sound economic idea. It is a little like each of us contracting never to take out a mortgage to buy a home or a second mortgage to tide us over during a period of career interruption or major illness. It would certainly bring some discipline to the family budget, but it could also make life very difficult—perhaps impossible. Yet many Americans, especially in the media, expect the government to do just that—to contract never to borrow money for the future. We can only hope our leaders develop the wisdom of Solomon before these non-economists talk our country into another depression.

On a more hopeful note, with all the recent talk about a political revolution in Washington, even the plans of those most worried about the deficit would probably affect economic growth only one-tenth as much as the typical recession, which recurs every five or six years. Six hundred politicians in Washington may have considerable power to divide our economic pie and some power to decide the quality of the ingredients that go into that pie. But 260,000,000 Americans still decide how large that pie will get as they decide how much of their paycheck to save at the end of each week. That is the yeast that makes the loaf bigger for the future. Even if we have lost faith in our politicians— which might be a good thing—there is no reason to lose hope in ourselves if we have got our own act together.

In the near future, I believe, several longtime pessimists will decide the economy is looking better because they will finally notice that the federal government has been getting relatively smaller for some time. But don't let their newfound optimism encourage you to make imprudent financial decisions. After all, the U.S. stock market is 4000 points higher than when John spoke more than a decade ago and he told Louis Rukeyser in early 1996 that "It's time to be cautious about U.S. stocks." It's a little late to suddenly become wildly enthusiastic about our stock market when it is simply beginning to reflect economic reality.

TAKING THE LOG FROM YOUR OWN EYE ...

We live in a credit economy and an advertising culture that advises us to buy now and pay later. At best, this is a dubious proposition. The underlying philosophy—a dangerous one—is that we accept gratification before we've earned it."

Sir John M. Templeton

Despite living a debt-free lifestyle, John is hardly paranoid about the federal debt. Most Americans are just the opposite. We continue to pile debt on our homes, cars, and credit cards, while we criticize our political leaders for doing the same thing with the federal debt. The media virtually never mention it, but our corporate and personal debt today is approaching the $10 trillion mark—twice the level of our federal debt! And corporate debt has been declining relative to our national income, which means individual Americans are piling up more and more consumer debt. Even so, as with the federal debt, we aren't facing a crisis since interest rates have declined, many people pay their cards off each month, and our incomes are stable or rising, which in turn means our payments are manageable in relation to our income. But the trend is still hardly a formula for financial or spiritual success.

The average American now carries four credit cards and is solicited for six more each year. Do you remember when we all thought that we piled up consumer debt only because the government encouraged us to by allowing a tax deduction for the interest we paid on our credit card debt? Have we become more virtuous since the devilish government stopped making us do it? Of course not. Fortunately, there are at least some encouraging signs that we're trying to get a grip.

As an investment counselor, you learn to watch popular trends. I offer a recent article from *Reader's Digest*, called "That's Outrageous," as a sign of hope regarding our improving attitudes toward debt. The article was subtitled: "Spotlighting Absurdities in Our Society Is the First Step Toward Eliminating Them." It said:

> James Douglas Nichols has made clear his disdain for the United States government, but that did not stop him from collecting $89,950 in subsidy checks from the U.S. Department of Agriculture. That was between 1986 and 1992—before he was held, and subsequently released, in connection with the April 19, 1995, Oklahoma City bombing that killed 168 and wounded at least 490. Nichols' younger brother, Terry, who has also been held in connection with the bombing, had odd ideas about what many accept as the American way of life as well. He mocked U.S. currency as worthless. In his mind that seems to have justified using credit cards to rack up more than $31,000 in unpaid bills. Chase Manhattan Bank won a $17,861 judgment against him in January 1993. In 1992, another credit-card company also won a suit against Nichols, for $13,691 in unpaid Visa bills.[4]

It would be easy to dismiss these guys as radical. Yet in many ways, they are vivid examples of states of mind addressed by the *Economist* in a recent cover story called "The Decadent Puritans," which stated that too many of us have embraced "an odd combination of ducking responsibility and telling others what to do."

Take, for example, the case of Harry Figgie and Peter Grace, co-chairmen of the Grace Commission established by President Reagan, the purpose of which was to offer ideas on cutting government waste.

After completing his work on the commission, Figgie wrote his best-seller, *Bankruptcy 1995*, which *Forbes* magazine said bore "only a resemblance to true economics." In the book, Figgie insisted that our politicians would bankrupt our country by piling up federal debt, and lots of people bought his thinking. Of course, 1995 has come and gone, and the U.S. economy still looks pretty good—although Figgie's own company hasn't been quite as fortunate. As the *Wall Street Journal* reported,

> Figgie International Chairman Harry Figgie, Jr., in his bestselling book *Bankruptcy 1995: The Coming Collapse of America and How To Stop It*, sounds the alarm about America's penchant for living on a 'champagne appetite and a beer income.' But that's precisely the kind of diet on which Mr. Figgies's own company has indulged itself in recent years, according to allegations in a shareholder lawsuit filed by a former executive.[5]

The article went on to detail the obvious irony: while Figgie's book was stirring up contempt for our government and its debt, Figgie International was struggling under a mountain of corporate debt and was busily preparing bankruptcy papers.

Then there is Peter Grace, Figgie's partner on the commission. Shortly before his death, Grace was ousted from his own company for, among other things, lavishing exorbitant perks on family members who were employed there. Ironically, these inefficiencies were noted by Wall Street analysts for several years while Mr. Grace served on the commission to make the government operate more smoothly.

Grace and Figgie were both capable and respected men, but their misfortunes demonstrate that large institutions take on personalities and lives of their own. You would expect such men to understand that an organization as large and complex as the federal government might experience similar problems, despite the best intentions of other capable and respected men.

The moral is that the best thing we can do for our economy is to practice sound business principles ourselves rather than ranting about the evils of the government.

As paranoia over the deficit moved into high gear around 1992, Robert Bartley, the editor of the *Wall Street Journal*, wrote a book called *The Seven Fat Years*. He is hardly a liberal, and yet, in a chapter called "The Dread Deficit," he wrote:

> The deficit is not a meaningless figure, only a grossly overrated one.... The deficit has no detectable effect on interest rates ... nor

is what we call "the deficit" an appropriate or particularly meaningful measure of the "burden we are leaving our grandchildren." . . .
Our politicians have conjured the deficit into a bogeyman with which
to scare themselves. In symbolizing the bankruptcy of our political
process, the deficit has become a great national myth with enormous
power. But behind this political symbol, we need to understand the
economic reality, or lack of it. . . . In the advanced economic litera-
ture, the big debate is over whether deficits matter *at all.*

With a similar grasp of economic reality, David Stockman, President Reagan's budget director, was a lone voice in the wilderness during the early 1980s when he said that tax cuts and increased defense
spending would make our deficits balloon. He was right. Our annual
budget deficits soared to 5.5% of our national income during the mid-
eighties. So you'd think the media and politicians would be most interested when he declared the problem was behind us. Not so. Our nation
has continued to be obsessed with budget deficits even after Stockman's views were updated in the *Wall Street Journal* on January 31, 1994:

> In what Mr. Stockman himself described as "a reversal of the
> gloom and doom I've last espoused," he is now predicting that the fed-
> eral deficit will shrink even faster than the White House projects. . . .
> Mr. Stockman projected that the deficit—which now amounts to
> about 3.4% of gross domestic product—will fall to about 1.5% by the
> end of the decade. . . . Mr. Stockman now says there isn't any need
> for another round of deficit reduction. . . . In his remarks Friday, he
> said, "We didn't know it at the time, but the 1980s amounted to an
> epochal race between the U.S. and the USSR over who could reach
> fiscal bankruptcy. They got there first. . . ."

In essence, Stockman was echoing what John has been saying for
years. The reality is that the Cold War is over, and that fact has tremendous ramifications for our federal deficit and economy. Yet perceptions
have yet to catch up due to political rhetoric.

Actually, Stockman was too pessimistic in his projections, for we've
reached his target much earlier than even he anticipated. In late 1995
and early 1996, as our politicians shut down our government during the
budget battle, the *Economist* wrote: "Rich country governments have
improved their housekeeping in the past four years. The main reason
is economic recovery. . . . America's government, if it ever re-opens,
should run up a deficit of 1.5% of GDP this year."[6] To clarify that, put

Federal Deficit as a percentage of GDP

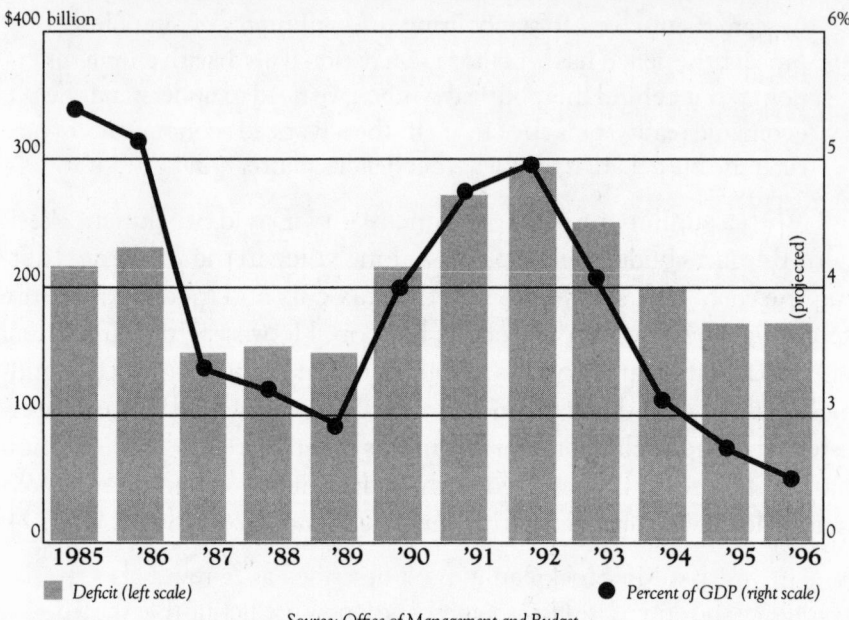

Deficit (left scale)   Percent of GDP (right scale)

Source: Office of Management and Budget

it in the context of your family's finances. Imagine your family income is about $40,000 (the national average), 1.5% of which is $600. Now imagine what would happen to your family if it "shut down" every time you and your spouse disagreed about whether or not to spend that money. It might start a war!

WAR AND OUR FEDERAL DEBT

There was a time during the Second World War when the federal debt was much worse in relation to our gross domestic product than now, when it was not clear we would survive as a nation.[7]

Sir John M. Templeton

One advantage of being graced with more than eighty years on this planet, as Sir John Templeton has been, is that you see how history repeats itself. Younger people, who often seem most pessimistic about our federal debt, usually have a more limited view of history. Their knowledge of the federal debt usually dates back to about the time the Cold War entered its final stages during the early eighties.

Yet in some ways, even these young worriers can be forgiven for over-reacting. Like most Americans, they don't realize that America was at war during that time. While most wars are hard to miss, this one was fortunate, as wars go, in that no bombs were dropped. It was a war of ideas and economics, as explained in a wonderful book by Peter Schweizer called *Victory*. In the introduction he says:

> In early 1982, President Reagan and a few key advisers began mapping out a strategy to attack the fundamental economic and polit-ical weaknesses of the Soviet system. "We adopted a comprehensive strategy that included economic warfare, to attack Soviet weak-nesses," recalls Casper Weinberger (President Reagan's Secretary of Defense). "It was a silent campaign, working through allies and using other measures.[8]

Obviously many things contributed to the collapse of the Soviet economy, but the point is that we conservatives often claim credit for that victory. And we should. But we too often neglect to explain that the cost of that victory contributed to the debt explosion of the eight-ies. It might therefore benefit all of us to reflect on a story printed in the February 1996 edition of *Worth* magazine, which is associated with the Fidelity Mutual Funds:

> Considering that our federal budget still bears the scars of the defense buildup of the 1980s, it's worth knowing how much of this spending was truly necessary—not to lay blame on its critics or pro-ponents, but to better understand the consequences of our decisions as a nation. Increasingly, the spending of that time colors the polit-ical debate in this country, and has no small effect on how many of us arrange our financial lives.... [Economist Walter] Mead's story "The Two Trillion Dollar Mistake" persuasively argues that fear blinded our decision making in the 1980s, causing us to waste valuable resources that could have been put to more productive use. Mead's history les-son won't be easy for many of us to accept, but like all valuable lessons, it is ignored at some peril.

I found Walter Mead's article "The Two Trillion Dollar Mistake" well worth a trip to the library. Though I don't agree with all of his views, Mead, the son of the well known church consultant Loren Mead, does indicate that there are three important reasons for us to set parti-san politics aside long enough to enlighten ourselves about what truly happened in the eighties.

First, a mental victory parade might do wonders for the American spirit. The Cold War ended with a whimper instead of a bang, which psychologically leaves all of us feeling a little empty. When my father returned from World War II, economic conditions were difficult, but the victory celebration that followed left little doubt that the war was over and that better days certainly lay ahead. But after winning the Cold War, we never really celebrated on a national level.

Second, such a celebration might do wonders to bring together this community we call America. I was startled when the confused producer of the economic video I mentioned earlier actually called John and me "liberals" simply because we understood that things looked better now that the war was over. Falsely labeling people is *not* a good way to win friends and influence people. It is bad enough that we divide people into liberals and conservatives. Believing that true conservatives must be pessimists divides us even further. Ronald Reagan certainly wouldn't understand it.

Finally, we should understand that while the Cold War may have been silent and strange, it was also expensive. The *Economist* recently detailed that defense spending soared from about $150 billion per year in 1981 to about $300 billion per year by 1985—the period during which Stockman preached his "doom and gloom." To put that in perspective, that difference is roughly equivalent to the projected budget deficit for 1996.

Defense spending has fallen during the nineties. I will not enter the political debate about whether that is good or bad, but economically, it has helped to reduce our budget deficit. Considering our strengthening economy, the disappearance of the savings-and-loan problem (which wasn't a "crisis" after all), and the slowing rate of growth in social programs, Empower America estimated last year's deficit at under $170 billion. While that may still be too high, it is about a quarter of what many pessimists had forecast during the early nineties.

Our local, state, and federal governments now spend a lower percentage of our GDP than virtually any major nation. Our deficit is actually the second lowest of the major nations. Only Norway's is lower. By comparison, two of our major trading partners, Canada and Great Britain, have deficits well over twice as large in relation to their incomes.[9]

The important point is this: most of the pessimistic investors I counsel believe that the debt buildup of the eighties was due solely to domestic social spending by liberals. Much of this spending continues, of course, as people continue to become unemployed, grow sick, and, especially, live longer than before. This makes the future appear uncertain. But for those who understand that the deficits were also due to the Cold War, which is now over, the future looks considerably brighter.

THIS TOO SHALL PASS

To the shrimp and seaweed tossed by combers, swirled in the backwash and drowned in the breakers, life may seem confusing. But to the big thinker standing on the beach with his schedule of ocean tides, the pattern of the waves is plain.

J. Bottum, *First Things*

When trying to understand something as complex as the federal debt, it is easy to feel like a shrimp in the backwash, but there are relatively simple patterns to the waves of federal debt. Understanding them will give us the confidence that we and our children are not about to drown in a sea of red ink and despair. Broadly, these economic waves reflect

Ratio of the Gross Federal Debt to GNP

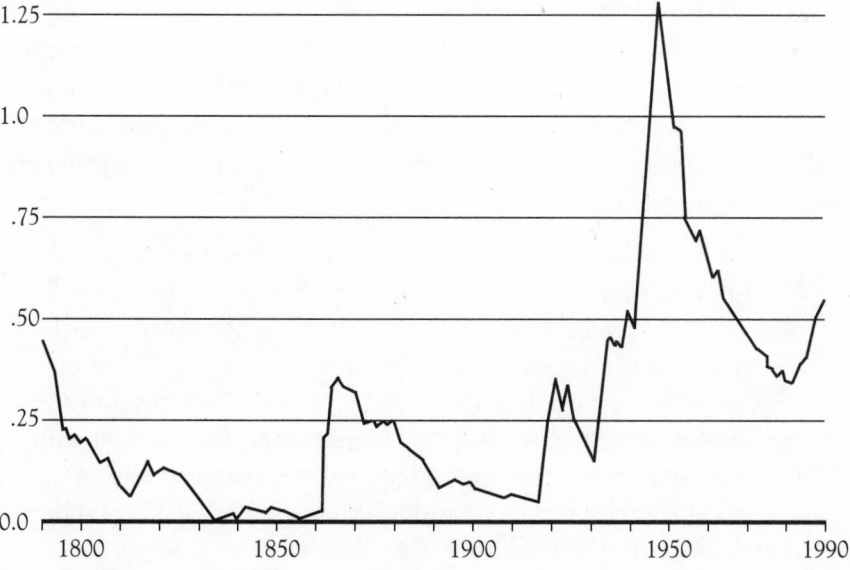

times of war and peace. The chart on the previous page shows America's federal debt for each decade leading up to our own.

As you can see, America began its life as a nation with a huge debt after the Revolutionary War. As in most wars, our government borrowed money to buy the things it needed to conduct a war. The same thing happened during the Civil War, World War I, and especially World War II when our annual deficit reached the equivalent of $600 billion, more than three times today's deficit. (Note that during the Vietnam War, we printed money rather than borrowing it, which produced inflation rather than debt.)

You need this long-term perspective because many people fret when they read statistics that show how the federal debt has doubled in relation to our income since 1980, and it leads them to feel quite pessimistic. But economic history shows that the debt was astronomical in 1946, fell to one-fourth that level by 1980, and has crept back up to only one-half of its all-time record. Concern is an appropriate response to this situation—but pessimism and paranoia are not.

Was the spending that caused this debt worth it? We might feel better knowing that it was. In the words of the *Wall Street Journal*, "We would certainly argue that winning the World War was worth borrowing 100% of our GDP, and winning the Cold War was worth borrowing 50%."[10]

So why do politicians remain so obsessed with the deficit? First, it is a problem that needs to be addressed. Still, most of the rhetoric can be explained by the old political proverb: "Don't waste time trying to start a parade. Find a parade, jump in front, and take credit for leading it."

In this land of more than 250 million people, it is actually quite difficult for 500 politicians to change our economy in a very significant way. As the *Economist* recently observed,

> No British budget is complete, for example, without another carefully considered change in the relative taxation of different kinds of alcoholic beverage. Such is active government. America's constitution allows even greater scope for activity as an end in itself. Changes in domestic policy have to be approved by both Senate and House of Representatives, which facilitates the conceit that the House has done this or the Senate that (make a Contract with America, pass a budget), when next to nothing has actually happened. The same is true of the White House, only more so.[11]

This very glacial system is what the Founding Fathers had in mind with their various checks and balances. Still, both political parties like to appear as if they are the only ones who can save Western Civilization from this apparent crisis. President Clinton wanted us to let him change "the economy, stupid," and one influential (and very young) Republican congressman said after the House passed the budget act in the fall of 1995, "We have met our goal. In seven years we will in fact balance the budget, save the country, and save the next generation."

My personal opinion is that if the United States doesn't soon experience a moral and spiritual reawakening, both of these politicians—and their parties—will have trouble explaining to future generations what went wrong. Interestingly, a recent survey of thousands of college-bound students found that their primary worry was not the economy or the deficit, but the moral condition of the country. It might be wise for a political leader to point out that there is relatively little he can do about personal morality.

Of course, I would expect most politicians—who rarely lack ego—would challenge my analysis. They remind me a bit of the fictional hero Don Quixote, who imagined that windmills were actually giants with whom he had to do battle. Yet when the blades of the windmill brought him back to reality by knocking him on his backside, instead of admitting the truth, Quixote further imagined that a magician had somehow turned the giants into windmills "in order to deprive me of the glory of overcoming them." Mortals who imagine themselves to be the saviors of civilization are more abundant in our humanistic culture than ever, but their outsized egos and imaginations can be shadowy distractions to you on your journey to spiritual and financial success.

Also, too many politicians, of whatever political party, seem to believe that anger and confusion among our citizens is a small price to pay for putting our society on a smoother road into the future. Of course, the idea that a society benefits at the expense of its individual citizens was precisely the argument of communist leaders. I'm not sure "the end justifies the means" can ever be a route to the promised land in a democracy—or anywhere else, for that matter. We need more leaders with a clearer vision of a better end and a better means of getting there, especially about our federal debt.

The Latest Scoop on the Federal Debt

The February 10, 1996, edition of the *Economist*, had this to say about the Federal debt in a special study:

> An individual who borrows to finance higher spending must lower future spending to repay the debt. Many assume that this applies to governments too, so that a national debt is bound to impoverish future generations. . . . This is often a misconception.
>
> There are good reasons for trimming budget deficits, which can impose heavy burdens on an economy. Yet the simple conclusion that a generation which inherits a national debt of, say, 50% of GDP is bound to be better off than one which inherits a national debt of, say, 100% is confused—and often wrong.

The study in the *Economist* contained a chart called "The High Cost of War," which showed that Federal debts usually rise during war and that Great Britain survived a debt-to-income ratio of about 240% at the end of World War II, when America's soared to 128%.

The *Economist* concluded:

> Today's generation would not thank its predecessors if, seeking to avert a national-debt "burden," they had failed to win these wars. . . . A national debt that finances welfare at the expense of private investment could be a burden; one that finances a new road network—or wins a war—may be a boon. . . . A fairer way of looking at things might be to say that, in so far as a national debt reduces the productive capital that one generation hands on to its successors, it is merely trimming the size of an already massive legacy. That hardly constitutes a "burden," in any sense of the word.

DEBT VERSUS INCOME

While no single statistic can capture the reality, one of the best measures is the trend of outstanding debt as a portion of yearly output. . . . A meaningful and achievable fiscal objective would be to get the trend of outstanding debt headed back down as a percentage of GDP. This would not

*require a balanced budget, only that the deficit shrink in proportion to a grow-
ing economy, as it did from 1945 to 1974.*

Wall Street Journal (November 18, 1994)

Although the discussion that follows may not be the most entertaining one in this book, it is one of the most enlightening. So please
stick with me. I'll make it as simple as possible.

A handful of influential commentators do not agree with John and
the *Wall Street Journal* that it is helpful to compare our debt to our
national income. They want us to look only at the debt, or negative,
side of America's balance sheet.

For example, consider my friend Larry Burkett. He is a financial commentator whose opinions can be heard every day on a thousand Christian radio stations across the country. He has written a best-seller about
the federal debt that was apocalyptic in its prophecies. He is respected
by my more conservative clients, and many conservative ministries
disseminate his views. I respect him a great deal, for he has helped thousands of people better understand budgeting, credit-card management,
and other matters of personal finance. And he is one of the few American leaders I know of who seems capable of disagreeing with you in a
genuinely loving spirit. For that I am most grateful.

But for several years I have disagreed, often publicly, with him for
writing that comparing debt to income is "irrelevant" and that those
who do so are "confused." Even the slightly more optimistic Pat Robertson has written: "The key indicator to look at is the federal debt in relation to our national output, what is called the debt/GNP ratio."[12] (GDP
and GNP are roughly analogous and can be interchanged for the purposes of this book.)

In his book *The Coming Economic Earthquake*, Burkett wrote:

> In the last several years a new "theory" has been developed in
> Washington that the national debt really doesn't matter since it is a
> smaller ratio of the country's gross national product (GNP) than it
> was thirty years ago. That is not true. In 1980, the GNP was $2.7 tril-
> lion and the total debt was $914 billion.[13]

From that paragraph, you can understand why I spend a lot of time
explaining basic economics to denominational leaders who would like
to lift the spirits of their congregations. First, I don't know of a single
economist who believes the debt "really doesn't matter." At the very

least, most understand that debt can become politicized and spiritually destructive, which can't be good for our economy. Therefore, most agree that our economy would be better off without it. But neither do I know of a single leading economist who believes it is as serious an economic problem as Burkett has suggested over the years.

In a publication that Burkett promotes, I once wrote that the national debt is like "a bug on the windshield—unsightly and in need of removal, but hardly enough to stop the progress of American capitalism." To understand why, notice that Burkett begins his statistics with 1980. Pat Robertson did the same thing in his discussion of what he ominously called "The Debt Time Bomb."[14] Harry Figgie and other best-selling pessimists have basically focused our attentions on the same time frame. Why? Because it makes our government look as irresponsible as possible.

Other communicators have taken up the distracting illusion until most conservatives accept it as the truth. I regularly meet with conservative clients who have built their economic worldviews on this limited sense of history. Many have not made seriously needed investments because of it. Others have unwisely liquidated entire portfolios. Some have even left our country for what they believe is the greener pasture of other nations. Yet as General Patton liked to say, "If everyone is thinking alike, then somebody isn't thinking."

The truth is that the debt/GDP ratio *was* just as high thirty years ago, and was considerably *higher* just a few years before that. But when Burkett begrudgingly acknowledged the ratio, he ignored the years when it was as bad or worse. Yet he is far from alone in simply deleting those years from American economic history. Again, Pat Robertson followed suit in his discussion in *The New Millennium*. They choose 1980 as the near-utopian ideal since that's the date that makes the debt windmill look more like the giant they would have us imagine it to be.

My basic disagreement with Burkett is over what he terms the "new theory" developed by "Washington" (that is, the idea that we gain a more realistic view of the economy by looking at debt as a percentage of GDP). While virtually any idea can be discredited among us conservatives today by insinuating that it was created in "Washington," most private economists have long disagreed with Burkett and the conservative politicians on this one. John did so back in 1984. Most Americans would too if they thought about it for a minute.

THE BALANCED PERSPECTIVE

The optimist has the power of seeing things in their entirety and in their right relations. The pessimist looks from a limited and a one-sided point of view. The one has his understanding illuminated by wisdom, the understanding of the other is darkened by ignorance. Each is building his world from within, and the result of the building is determined by the point of view of each.

Ralph Waldo Trine

That sentiment was published over a hundred years ago, though it is helpful advice for those today who worry over the federal debt.

As I travel around the country, I often begin my seminars by asking if anyone knows the size of the federal debt. Many people do. Then I ask them who we borrowed that debt from. Virtually no one knows. Then I ask how the debt relates to our nation's annual income. Again, very few have any idea. I then ask how the debt relates to our nation's assets. I have yet to find one person who knows. In essence, the vast majority of Americans focus on the negative side of America's balance sheet, which means, on a spiritual level, we no longer count our blessings.

Assume you are a loan officer fresh out of banking school, and your first job is to review an application for a mortgage loan of $60,000. The only thing you know is the size of the loan request and that the applicant has no income or assets. Do you grant the loan? Not if you are looking forward to a career as a loan officer.

But what if the applicant has an annual income of $100,000? In that case, you'd probably grant the loan, since most banks routinely approve mortgage loans up to two and a half times a person's annual income. In this particular example, most banks would probably lend the applicant as much as $250,000.

A few people, like John, might argue that the applicant would be better off to postpone the purchase until he or she could save enough to pay cash for the new home. But during the borrowing binge of the 1980s— or today—most people would not think of delaying the purchase. Few of us would even consider a $60,000 mortgage to be a terrible burden for someone with such a large income—or for that person's heirs.

My point is that to get a balanced perspective on this debt, you need to consider both the size of the debt *and* the income of the applicant. While it's common practice in millions of business transactions every day, few Americans apply the same principle to the federal debt. Most serious economists, however, do not make that mistake. While they are aware and concerned that our total accumulated debt is about $5 trillion (because politicians and the media keep reminding them), still, they keep in mind that our *annual* national income is over $7 trillion. That's good news, although few Americans seem to understand it.

Now, here is the important part: in the example given above, our applicant's ratio of debt to income is 60% ($60,000 debt on a $100,000 income). That ratio is right in the middle of the 50% to 70% that economists calculate as our present federal debt to national income ratio.

By comparison, the average American family's debt-to-income ratio was about 115% in the spring of 1995—an all-time high. So I was rather surprised when columnist Cal Thomas recently wrote: "Republicans have circled 2002 as the magic date when supposedly we will see politicians acting like average Americans: not spending what they don't have." Let's hope not! America might be better off if the average citizen borrowed money more like the government! And yet most lending institutions seem willing to take our personal borrowing to even higher levels.

In short, if the federal government were an average citizen seeking a mortgage loan, most banks might be willing to lend it four times the amount it has already borrowed. Of course, that would be foolish. (Yet we should remember that Great Britain's debt/income ratio was 240% at the end of World War II, but it survived as the ratio fell in the coming decades.) But the fact that in the past our nation's debt-to-income ratio has been twice today's level would surely indicate that we shouldn't grow paranoid—especially if we are simply trying to convince ourselves that public-sector borrowing must be restrained so that private consumers and corporations can pile up even more debt.

And I often wonder if that isn't what the argument is really all about. Even Larry Burkett, who sometimes quotes the Grace Commission as though it were the Great Commission, wrote in *The Coming Economic Earthquake*:

> The competition between the government and businesses for available funds is a real concern for most economists who understand that the total funds available to both the public and private sectors are limited. The more money the government pulls out of the system to feed its own spending, the less that is available for businesses. Since only the government can support the enormous deficits it has, businesses are in constant jeopardy of losing their source of capital. . . . The more the government siphons off, the less that is available for all others.

In essence, the competition between government and private-sector borrowing would be of little concern if we all adopted the same debt-free philosophy that John used to build his modest lifestyle and expansive mutual-fund business. Capitalism obviously needs roads, dams, G.I. bills, and other services to thrive. We Christians need to be especially careful that those of us who favor the private sector don't build a theology of selfishness in the name of biblical principles.

TRENDS IN INCOME

Statistics will show you that in my lifetime of eighty-one years, the standard of living has quadrupled after adjusting for inflation. Because these forces of progress are more forceful now than ever, our studies would indicate that a quadrupling may occur in as little as forty years. So how overwhelmingly grateful every one of us should be that God allowed us to be born in this blossoming time of civilization.[15]

Sir John M. Templeton

As a wise loan officer, you would also make sure that the applicant's income is not a one-time event. Ideally, you would like to see a history of reasonably increasing income over the past several years. In this situation again, America would be a strong applicant.

The *Wall Street Journal* recently published an important special section about the last half of the twentieth century. I saved it as a breathtaking glimpse of what has happened to America's economic life since I was born in 1950. One chart showed the Dow Jones Industrial Average has soared from around 250 to over 5000. Another showed that the percentage of people attending college has soared from around 4% back then to over 31% today. This is crucial because college graduates now make approximately twice as much over their lifetimes as noncollege graduates.

Yet the most impressive chart showed that our national income (adjusted for inflation) has roughly *tripled*. It also showed our after-tax, inflation-adjusted income *per person* has soared over tenfold during that time.[16] Did you know that the top tax bracket on dividends and income was over 80% in 1950 but is about half that today?

I realize that many media personalities and politicians lament the recent slowdown in wages. But as the *Economist* has pointed out:

After-tax per-capita income
in thousands of 1985 dollars

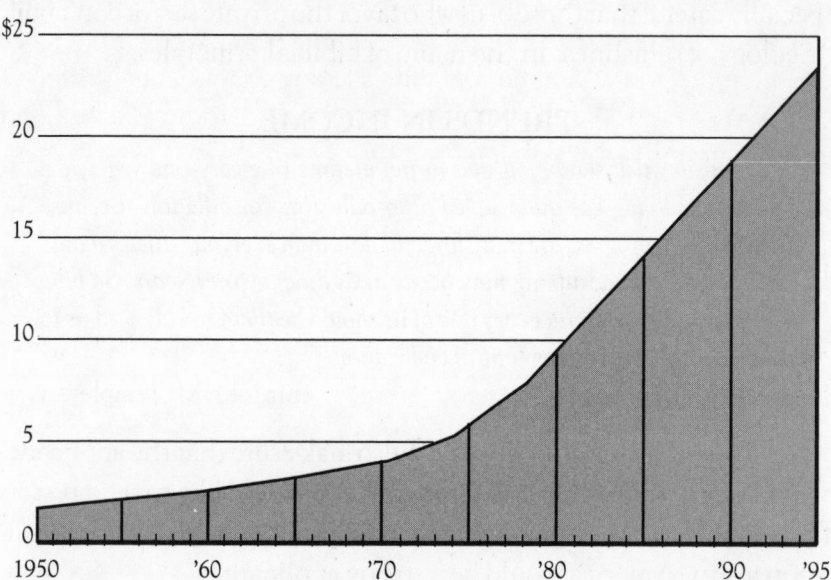

During the 1960s and early 1970s, wage increases far exceeded gains in labor productivity, as strong unions were able to extract unsustainable wage concessions from their employers. During the 1980s and early 1990s, the combination of international competition and impressive productivity gains that outpaced wages appears to have brought wage levels back in line with reality. If so, workers may also begin to benefit from increases in labor productivity.[17]

Pessimists hate to point it out, but corporations enjoyed 20% profit margins in 1950. By 1980 they were down to 5%. They are back to 10% today. Yet most pessimists again act as though the world were created in 1980 so they increasingly talk about "corporate greed" even as they long for the job security of the "good old days" of the 50s and 60s.

But there are other reasons why few people feel rich today. One of the most important is the changing nature of our national income, though the *Economist* has again challenged that feeling with this fact: "American official statistics still have a big hole that leads them [economists] to underestimate the economy's health. The productivity of service industries is, most economists believe, grossly understated in the records."[18]

Also, the nature of our paychecks has changed. Since 1950, the total compensation of all American workers has averaged almost exactly two-thirds of our national income. The remainder goes as profits to those who provide the capital to finance our factories, transportation companies, and so on. But in 1950, actual paychecks amounted to about 60% of our national income. Benefits accounted for about 5% more. Today, our paychecks reflect less than 55% of our national income and benefits amount to more than 10%.[19]

Much of this increase in benefits has been because benefits are often tax-advantaged, and many of them have been somewhat hidden. Think what health-care benefits alone have done to those figures. Most financial counselors know how surprised thousands of retiring blue-collar workers have been in recent years to receive lump-sum pension distributions worth hundreds of thousands of dollars. Few felt rich, but many were.

REAL FAMILY INCOME

The late 1950s and early 1960s—Mickey Mantle's golden era—was truly an era of security and hope. . . . But perhaps life in the Mantle era became too comfortable. Like spoiled children who whine louder with each new toy, young Americans rejected the good life in favor of pursuing the perfect life—the most dangerously childish notion there is.[20]

David Asman

Another chart in the *Wall Street Journal*'s fifty-year study explained another reason why our pessimistic friends sound right when they claim that "median family income has been stagnant"—despite the fact that our national and individual wealth has actually soared. It has more to do with the changing nature of the American family than with family income. The chart showed that in 1950 only 9.1% of American families were headed by a single parent (that is, divorced, never married, or widowed). Today that figure is 24.75%. This is terribly important to understand.

Imagine that Joe makes $30,000 a year and his wife, Jane, also makes $30,000. Their family income is then $60,000. Now, assume that Joe and Jane get a divorce. If, after their divorce, both Joe and Jane get $5,000 raises and now make $35,000 each, what happens to our statistics of *family* income? It *drops* by more than 40% because there are now twice as many families! That may sound simplistic, but divorce alone is a large, though neglected, factor in the gloomy assessments of the pessimists. It makes me wonder why we conservatives, who talk most about the breakdown of the American family, are most likely to use *family* income as our standard of national success. And we might note that as unemployment has plummeted, the new workers often earn the lowest wages. So our actual success can actually *lower* the average income of *working* Americans.

Still, I believe there is one legitimate reason to feel discouraged about the American family—our low personal savings rate. Though somewhat understated, since it doesn't include the appreciation on our past savings, it is about half what it was twenty years ago and is widely documented as being among the lowest of the major nations. We Americans generally live more on the edge of fiscal solvency than we used to—and that makes me uncomfortable.

Over the years, I have come to believe that one of the greatest economic myths about Americans is that we love money. If we did, we would hold on to more of it. I suspect that what we truly love is possessions. There are so many wonderful toys we just have to have in order to feel better—but the more we buy, the less we save. The less we save, the worse we feel. The worse we feel, the more we go shopping. It is a vicious cycle—so vicious in fact, Czech president and philosopher Vaclav Havel has termed our condition "totalitarian consumerism."

If you have trouble believing these statistics are true, I suggest you simply conduct your own study by walking around your home and the homes of your friends. Note all the microwaves, can openers, garage door openers, computers, blenders, televisions, clothes dryers, and other items your parents could never have imagined. Then ask your parents about the size of their home when they were growing up. (In 1975, the average new home was 1,500 square feet; it is over 2,000 square feet today.) Ask them to describe the car they drove when they were first married, whether it had a tape player, cruise control, or air-conditioning. Ask if they even *dreamed* of owning two cars. The fact is, many of us are already living the American dream, even if we aren't aware of it.

UNCONSCIOUS WEALTH

The wealth of a nation is not to be found by asking a statistically significant, random sample of people to have a stab at it. What people think, still less what they say, is not a good guide to the way the world is. People don't know.[21]

The Economist

Again, imagine you are the lending officer evaluating America's mortgage. No doubt you would not only look closely at America's income but at its assets as well. Once again, most Americans are not aware of what our nation's assets are. Few people realize that our government has reserved title to about 30% of our land for our present and future use. According to the *Economist*, our federal government owns 70% of Alaska, 80% of Nevada, and almost 50% of California—and about 50% of our twelve western states put together.[22] Those lands contain vast natural and recreational resources.

Our government also holds about $400 worth of gold reserves for every American. I could go on and on about our collective blessings. The big picture, as the Bush administration once estimated, is this: America's total assets at that time were about $50 trillion.[23] It also estimated that our wealth had tripled since 1960, in real, inflation-adjusted dollars.

That is about $200,000 for each American. Yes, I know that sounds highly inflated to most of us, and it is also apparently true that 40% of our *private* wealth is owned by the wealthiest 1% (on the other hand, the wealthiest 5% of Americans only get half as much of our national income as they did in the early 1900s). Yet when the World Bank recently included intangible wealth—such as people's education that enables the conversion of natural resources into usable wealth—it estimated our per capita wealth as being $421,000!

Before our hearts will find greater peace, our minds must grasp the fact that the vast riches of our nation are held in three sectors: the private sector, the public sector, and the independent sector.

Private wealth belongs to individuals. It is typically the only wealth most of us even think about, although investment counselors often find that people rarely assess that wealth accurately. Most people have no idea how large their current or projected assets might be. For example, when reviewing estate plans, few of my clients list the value of the life insurance policies they have purchased over the decades. Retirement funds hold about 75% of our individual savings, but many are surprised at how the explosive stock market of 1995 increased the size of their accounts.

Public wealth is that which is held by local, state, and federal governments. Most of us never consider that we own an acre of Alaska, an ounce of gold in a government vault, a mile of interstate highway, part of an Air Force base, a few books in our public library, or the other forms of vast wealth held on our behalf by the government. While we are repeatedly reminded that our personal share of the federal debt is about $20,000, why are we never told that we share our federal assets as well?

The independent sector is even less appreciated. How many of us realize that we own a part of the churches we have contributed money to and their tens of billions of dollars in pension and endowment funds? How many of us realize that we own part of the buildings occupied by the Red Cross and other organizations? Who knows how much wealth is held by the great foundations of our land? It is virtually inestimable. Though each of these is very real wealth, we rarely understand that much of it enriches all of us, directly or indirectly, at some point in our lives.

Add the wealth in all these three sectors together (as the Bush administration did) and you arrive at approximately $50 trillion. I have read private estimates that the number may be as much as $100 trillion!

Now let's put these incredible blessings back into the understandable context of our mortgage example. Our $5 trillion debt on our $50 trillion assets is like a $10,000 mortgage on a $100,000 home. Most of us would gladly agree to a mortgage like that!

Ultimately, when you consider the following: America's annual income; the strong trend of its income; its history of managing debt; its fairly prudent use of debt; its debt/income ratio in comparison to other borrowers; and the size of our national assets—the U.S. begins to look like an extremely credit-worthy applicant. This may be why virtually every pessimist I know still wants to lend the government money by buying U.S. treasury bills, notes, and bonds.

Even Larry Burkett has written: "Many retirees need absolute security in their investments since the money they have cannot be replaced and they don't have the temperament to take risks. Usually government securities represent the best overall investment for them."[24]

Expecting "absolute security" from human government strikes me as a significant leap of faith, especially for conservatives. Consider too the fact we are financing growth of the government we seek to reduce, thereby working against our own best interests. We are not unlike the Israelites who were so afraid that the giants would keep them from the promised land that they refused to enter it without ever seeing a giant. In looking for security, we often actualize our own worst fears.

FOLLOW THE MONEY

If there is a poor man among your brothers in any of the towns of the land that the Lord your God is giving you, do not be hardhearted or tight-fisted toward your poor brother. Rather be openhanded and freely lend him whatever he needs.

Deuteronomy 15:7–8

More than a generation ago, *Forbes* magazine stated that the federal debt was about $400 per person and that taxes might soon "bankrupt" our nation. I keep that article in a file to remind myself just how long people can live in fear and anxiety, as well as miss out on financial success, over a problem that is a fairly normal part of modern life.

Surely, one of the great mysteries is, "Why do I keep hearing all these dire predictions about the federal debt and its cost but nothing ever seems to happen?" Some people even seem to believe it is immoral and bound to arouse the wrath of God. Yet a careful study of Moses' life indicates he understood that it is no mystery that lending among neighbors can be a prudent and moral activity. Caspar Weinberger, President Reagan's secretary of Defense and the current chairman of *Forbes*, connected those concepts as deficit paranoia reached its peak in 1992. Beneath the headline "The Federal Deficit: Is It All That Bad?" he wrote:

> It seems appropriate to examine in some detail the exact anatomy of this deficit, to try to determine why it is that, despite all the dire predictions, there have been no highly adverse blows to the economy that can be traced directly to the deficit.
>
> Why hasn't the deficit done more harm? Essentially the deficit simply requires another government payment program, this one going to the holders of government bonds—the people who lend money to the government to cover the gap between our revenues and expenditures. They are paid approximately $300 billion a year in interest.
>
> It is instructive to ask where this $300 billion a year goes. One myth is that we are surviving only because so many foreign countries buy our bonds. Actually, comparatively little interest goes abroad. The latest figures (for 1991) show that 12% of the national debt is owned by foreigners, which means that about 12% of our annual interest payments is paid to them. This figure has been remarkably consistent since 1980. . . .
>
> While the deficit is too high and it would be far better if less money had to be raised and paid out by the government in the form of interest, the effect of it is a different kind of government transfer

payment which ultimately brings more benefits to our economy than do many other government transfer and entitlement programs.[25]

Empower America recently updated its estimate of total interest payments as being $235 billion in 1995. Many economists believe they will go even lower. It is also worth pointing out that many of those interest payments are taxable, so a good portion of them returns to the Treasury at tax time.

As I write, our government has borrowed about $550 billion from foreigners. The interest checks amount to about $30 billion and are therefore about 0.5% of our national income. That is about what our casinos made off legal gambling last year and is far less than we annually spend on adult-rated movies and tobacco products. And we know some of that interest is reinvested back into America. So it should hardly be allowed to worry you unduly, keep you from investing for the future, or destroy your spiritual well-being.

Most people I counsel, and even some of the supposed experts I debate, believe our debt is owed to the Japanese and, to a lesser extent, other foreign nations. This can lead to resentment and further divisiveness. Yet as Weinberger said, that is simply another myth of American economic life. Unfortunately, that picture is largely painted by our fellow conservative politicians and popular media that take such illusions at face value. In an article titled "Debunking the Yellow Peril," the *Economist* said:

> What a waste of worry. First, the Japanese no longer hold anything like as many Treasury bonds as they once did, only about 3% of the total outstanding. Second, America no longer needs to rely on foreigners to finance its budget deficit, for during the 1990s the deficit has fallen and domestic savings have become available.[26]

The *Economist* isn't alone. When President Bush tallied up America's balance sheet, he included only about one-tenth of our federal debt as a liability because almost 90% of it has been borrowed from fellow Americans. That is a terribly important fact. Three thousand years ago Moses understood that it is a moral thing for a nation's people to lend to one another, but it is another thing for them to borrow too much from the people of other nations. That kind of borrowing could become a burden for future generations.

Like Moses, Abraham Lincoln also understood a thing or two about debt. As the debt grew during the Civil War, he said: "The great advantage of citizens being creditors as well as debtors with relation to the public debt, is obvious. Men can readily perceive that they cannot be much oppressed by a debt which they owe to themselves."

We hear a great deal today about our country ceasing to function when the interest payments consume all the taxes our government collects. That could happen if our debt/income ratio were four times today's rate. Lincoln too probably heard such talk a century ago. As *Forbes* has explained, "The interest burden was very high after the Civil War. But the economy survived. And today's interest burden is dwarfed by federal receipts." The article went on to detail that even though government was much smaller in Lincoln's day, the interest payments on the debt were only about one-half of 1% less of our national income than they are today. They are about 3% today, where they have been for over ten years.[27] Ironically, if all our government could do was pay interest to Treasury bond holders, we might wonder if it would really bother many of the most vocal worriers!

If you are like most of my clients and friends, this bit of light will be very difficult to adjust to as the subject has been shrouded in darkness and illusion for a very long time. Unlike Moses and Lincoln, modern leaders rarely seem to differentiate between debt that is owed to ourselves and debt that is owed to others.

Still, Robert Eisner, a past president of the American Economic Association, believes we must see the difference. Disputing the media and politicians, he has denounced the spiritual and financial harm done by the "political paranoia about budget deficits and government debt." In an article called "The Grandkids Can Relax," he wrote these words in the *Wall Street Journal*: "The government debt may be better viewed as an *asset* of the American public, its predominant owners. We might say that each infant born today is given a nest egg of government savings bonds or Treasury bills, notes and bonds."[28]

In essence, Eisner may wish we didn't have a federal debt, but he also understands that few of us will lie awake worrying about being a burden on our grandchildren if we own $20,000 worth of Treasury securities that are paying us interest. In fact, he understands we might feel the exact opposite once we truly understand what Treasury securities are. While many of us believe government never creates wealth and should therefore never borrow, as corporations do, he knows that our government has borrowed from us to make many productive investments in such things as winning the Cold War, reserving vast natural resources for future generations, educating and healing our citizens, and much more. He understands that those of us who have saved and loaned money for those investments receive the interest from other Americans for having done so. And he understands that most of what we have heard about this complex matter "only compounds the confusion about the vital issue of providing for our future."

My personal experience confirms his conclusion. I am constantly surprised by how many retired clients begin our conversation with, "The government is going to ruin our economy by paying out all that interest." They then ask, "Do you think I'll ever get enough interest from my savings bonds and Treasury securities again?"

Many who invest in certificates of deposit rather than Treasuries don't understand that most banks use a large percentage of our deposit to buy Treasury securities. That means a significant portion of the interest we get from the bank is from what we ourselves often call "wasteful government interest expense that doesn't benefit anyone."

Many of these people are retirees whose livelihoods depend very heavily on the interest. It therefore amuses me when Florida politicians demonize the interest expense. It is quite possible that no state in the union has benefited more from the government paying interest on the debt than my state where so many retirees live.

Most of us can be forgiven for not understanding these issues. We have seen that there are very few people who really want to enlighten us about the world of political economics. Yet I think we have a right to expect more from our moral leaders. Far too often we get the kind of confusing rhetoric that Pat Robertson offered in *The New Millennium*. In that book (p. 251), he writes, "Government does not produce anything. Government never creates wealth." Yet on the very next page he counsels, "People would be well advised to avoid the stock market until the smoke clears . . . and to have available investments of the safest and most liquid sort, such as U.S. Treasury bills. The government will never default."

It strikes me as appropriate that that advice was offered in a chapter called "The New Economics," for it is indeed new economics when we believe we can get government out of our lives but have it protect all our wealth, or invest only in government that "never creates wealth" but expect to enrich our children during the coming millennium.

Like far too many leaders, Robertson has been waiting for the smoke to clear—and feeling rather than thinking about economic matters—for a very long time. In 1983, he wrote a letter to an acquaintance who had sold all his stocks on Robertson's advice and then watched the market soar. The letter said:

> It is my *feeling* now, as it was last year, that the economy of the United States and the world is in an extremely precarious position. The banking system is overloaded with hundreds of billions of dollars worth of bad loans and any day there is a very real danger of a major default which could conceivably trigger a banking collapse. This will mean, when it comes, that the stock market is going to go down and that only the most liquid securities such as United States Treasury bills will prove to be good investments . . . although you missed a slight market run up, you still have your capital intact and a year from now you may have cause to rejoice that you were more cautious.

The saddest part of that episode was that my acquaintance was wondering if God had failed him because he had taken the advice of a leader he trusted.

It is not my intent to single out Pat Robertson for criticism. He has brought some serious political and economic issues into the public arena. But I have never understood why people seem to accept economic and investment advice from virtually anyone who has access to a microphone or a newspaper column.

The moral is simply this: we might do well not to rely on politicians and media personalities for investment advice. Rather, consider these words from Richard Mouw, president of Fuller Theological Seminary:

> We do not have a theology of public life yet. So in the political sphere, we went from unthinking noninvolvement to unthinking involvement. . . . We do have public spokespersons like Jerry Falwell and Pat Robertson, but they really haven't thought these issues through theologically. The result is that the theological basis for what their political followers have advocated has been at best minimal and at worst perverse.[29]

Often, the advice of such people is a shaky foundation on which to build a life of true success. Perhaps that is why James Sanders once wrote in *Torah and Canon* that "the true prophet does not engage in political diatribe to provide a rallying point for a particular course of action. . . . He questions all the powers that be in the name of the one power beyond them."

In many ways, Pat Robertson is simply a convenient metaphor for the many problems you face as an investor. As a former presidential candidate who remains active in politics, he should know that between the favorable debt/income ratios he shared in his book for 1929 and 1980, there was a far more troubling ratio for 1946 that he didn't quote—perhaps because it would have given his readers hope to see that things were actually much worse back then, yet we survived—even thrived. But, of course, that would not have angered them into the kind of political activism Robertson was hoping for.

As a media personality who can shape the perceptions of millions, Robertson's visions of a stock market decline for the eighties and perhaps even a crash for 1993 were careless at best and irresponsible at worst. They cost a lot of people a lot of money—money that might have been put to good use. It is now in the hands of more secular, and perhaps more productive stewards.

Most importantly, as a minister in the tradition of Moses and Jesus, Robertson should not rely on columnist George Will to remind us that "time was when American's savored freedom's uncertainties and considered 'security' an unworthy goal for free people."

THE TRUE WAY

Good times, hard times—this is what people keep saying. But let us live well, and the times shall be good. We are the times. Such as we are, such are the times.

St. Augustine

Unlike Pat Robertson, I believe it is futile to place our faith in government bonds while waiting for the smoke to clear. Americans need to see more clearly the direction to the promised land. They must be free of fear and confusion to confidently follow that vision. We must let our people go, not only politically, but mentally and spiritually.

Perhaps we could begin the journey by summarizing the economic landscape in the light of these facts: we Americans have a $10,000 mortgage on a $100,000 home, and $9,000 of that mortgage has been borrowed from family members who receive our interest payments.

The value of our home is far larger than any other home in the neighborhood. And it has been rising as few homes of its value ever have.

The debt-to-income ratio on our home stabilized years ago. We have an income that has supported a relatively much larger mortgage in the past. Our parents managed that larger mortgage through faith, work, and prudent investing in a common vision, rather than relying on anxiety-producing, highly partisan politics.

Finally, our income has been growing strongly in recent decades and has been, at worst, quite stable in recent years. We *can* afford to give for the social and moral development of our world. We *can* have the courage to prudently and ethically make the investments that will truly enrich our children well into the next millennium.

four

FIND
SAFETY IN NUMBERS

GOLDEN RULE:
Invest in many different places—there is safety in numbers

Put your
investments in
several places—
many places
even—because
you never know
what kind of bad
luck you are going
to have in this
world.
(*Ecclesiastes
11:2 GNB*)

Diversify. In stocks and bonds, as in much else, there is safety in numbers. So you must diversify, by company, by industry, by risk and by country.... Having said that, I should note that, for most of the time, most of our clients' money has been in common stocks.[1]

Sir John M. Templeton

Years ago, one of my clients merged his private company with a large multinational corporation. If anyone was financially secure, he was. He had received several million dollars' worth of the company's blue-chip stock, the dividends of which provided him an adequate income.

Like many small-business owners, virtually everything he had was invested in his business, but now, everything he had was invested in the new company's stock. Not only did his situation violate the portfolio theory that diversity is safer, it also violated the common-sense wisdom of my rural youth: "A man who names his pigs is broke and don't know it." In other words, don't get too attached to your investments. In more spiritual language, "Hold to the things of this world very lightly."

So during one of our initial meetings, I suggested he diversify his holdings, and I repeated this advice in several later meetings. He assured me that because this huge conglomerate was composed of several different types of businesses, it would never fail him. Besides, he said, he had made a pretty large capital gain in the stock. So he thought it wise to keep his eggs in one basket and watch it carefully.

For a while, his faith was justified. But one morning the company surprised Wall Street by announcing that it was reducing its dividend. It opened for trading a few hours later, down about 30% from the previous day's closing price. My multimillionaire client now had little income. So he was going to have to sell some stock, at prices 30% lower, and he would have to realize the capital gains anyway.

I wish this were an isolated example, but it is amazing how many Americans have bet incredible percentages of their wealth in direct contradiction to the counsel of those who advise diversity. While relatively few people concentrate on only one investment, as my client had done, more people make the same mistake by owning only one class of asset, such as favoring only certificates of deposit or bonds.

During the early 1980s, when six-month certificates of deposit paid over 15%, several of my retired clients told me there was no risk in government-guaranteed certificates paying those types of return. Therefore, despite my caution not to place so much faith in one asset class, some of them kept 100% of their assets in bank CDs. But within a few years of rolling them over at ever lower rates, their incomes had declined to the point where they were liquidating principle in order to live. And of course, they then understood there really was risk in *all*— repeat *all*—investments. Had they diversified into some other asset classes, they might have had some bonds with more stable income and some stocks that soared in value as interest rates fell.

To help you avoid that mistake, let me share a couple of simple planning tips. The first concerns how much you need to begin saving. If you haven't started saving yet, you should subtract the number twenty from your age and annually invest that percentage of your income until you can afford to retire. For example, if you are thirty, subtract twenty from your age and start saving 10% of your income each year. If you are forty, you need to save 20%. If you are fifty, 30%. And so on. Obviously, the earlier you start, the better.

The second tip concerns how much you should have in certificates of deposit, bonds, stocks, and other investments. Again, treat your actual age as a percentage. Place that percentage in something like certificates of deposit, fixed-rate annuities, or shorter-term bonds—investments that do not fluctuate greatly in value. Then invest the remaining percentage in stocks, real estate, and other assets that historically perform better than the other asset classes although they experience ups and downs along the way.

If you begin doing this when you are twenty years old, you will have 80% of your assets invested in growth investments for the long-term inflation protection you need. But if you are eighty years old, you will have only 20% of your assets subject to the ups and downs of the stock and real-estate markets.

If you are typical and have delayed saving for too long, I would resist the tendency to become too aggressive with your investing strategy later in life. I've usually found that is another case of two wrongs not adding up to one right.

Obviously, these are just rough guidelines that need to be tempered according to your personal philosophies about risk and return. But I have found them helpful places to begin thinking about asset allocation. Studies tell us that people spend far more time thinking about specific investments and where the markets are headed than about allocating assets. Yet the same studies also tell us a vast percentage of investors' returns (some studies say 90%) are due to asset allocation rather than the selection of specific investments or short-term market-timing decisions.

In short, for every person I meet who concentrates too heavily in one security or one asset class, or who expects to protect himself through market-timing, I counsel two who make the mistake of underinvesting in stocks—and three who make the mistake of not diversifying globally.

THE PRUDENT INVESTOR

There is a single company in Japan, the telephone company, whose market capitalization is greater than all the stocks in the whole nation of Canada or the whole nation of Germany. That stock is now selling for 120 times earn-

ings. We don't have a single share there.... Gradually the Japanese people
will send their money out of Japan to buy where the bargains are.
Sir John M. Templeton, *Outstanding Investor Digest*
(February 8, 1990)

When John said that, many of my clients were afraid the Japanese would soon own America and the world. Yet since that time, many Japanese stocks have declined by 50% or more before recovering some of the losses in recent months. This illustrates an important point: It is dangerous for an investor to place absolute faith in the fortunes of any single nation, regardless of how invincible it might seem at the time.

Like the Japanese, Americans have had to learn this lesson the hard way. From the excesses of the 1969 peak, most of our stocks declined about 50% in less than two years. Even our most sophisticated institutions thought the famous "Nifty Fifty" stocks of our largest corporations couldn't fail them. They had bid them up to eighty times earnings. That's about five times today's more normal valuations of around sixteen times earnings. By the time the market eventually bottomed in 1974, many of them had dropped by 80%. The famous Fidelity Magellan Fund dropped by 59% in 1973 and 1974 alone. Even the crash of 1987 was modest in comparison.

American investors learned some valuable lessons during those years, though few of my younger friends on Wall Street today can even tell you about that time. If history and human nature are still valid indicators, as I expect they are, most of the rest of us will eventually forget those lessons and have to relearn them once again. As I write, the stock market valuation of one American company, Microsoft, exceeds the stock market valuations of all companies in Denmark, Finland, and New Zealand combined.

Despite common perceptions in America, diversifying around the globe can actually lower your risk rather than increase it. The investment firm of Morgan Stanley did a famous study over twenty years that showed that if you had invested up to 40% of your stock market money internationally, you would have actually *decreased* your risk as you *increased* your return. Any percentage higher than that generally maintained the return but took on slightly higher risk, so there doesn't appear to be any reason to do it as a diversification measure—unless U.S. stocks become overvalued.

In a basic way, this makes sense. Consider oil. In the 1970s, the oil-producing countries of the Middle East, as well as Canada and Mexico, prospered as oil prices rose. Oil-consuming nations like the United States, however, were troubled by the trend. But in the 1980s, the trends reversed and the oil producers were troubled as the oil consumers prospered. So if an investor owned shares of an oil-producing company in Canada as well as an oil-consuming utility company in America, he would have diversified some of his risks away and enjoyed a smoother ride.

While most investors think they are safest by investing in CDs, Treasury bills, and other securities that don't fluctuate in value, those investments have been guaranteed losers over the long-term after inflation and taxes are considered. This is because all governments are under constant pressure to deliver more goods than people want to pay for. They will therefore visibly increase taxes or borrow money—or they might create new currency. The last usually leads to higher rates of inflation.

Sir John Templeton believes the best way to both prosper and minimize the ever-present risks of life is to diversify, as he explained in "Four Laws of Successful Investing," a speech published in the early nineties. He said, in part:

> A close approach to safety is diversification. That is, to diversify among types of assets, in many nations, including stocks of more than three dozen corporations in more than a dozen nations. That is the closest you can come to safety with your assets. . . . Right now it seems to me that one of the great mistakes is the desire of the American public to own too much of fixed income assets. To own cash, money market funds, certificates of deposit, or bond funds ignores the clear evidence that you will produce far better results in the long run by investing in equity securities. And yet today, the public has the most cash it has ever had in history. The average family has less than half as much in common stock in relation to its assets than it has had in the past. The great mistake, the great way people are fooling themselves today, is to think they can play it safe by holding cash reserves. They can't.

In essence, most of us still make the age-old mistake of confusing certainty with security. In the ancient story of the Israelites, one can almost hear the Hebrews celebrating their new-found freedom as they traveled out of Egypt and toward the Promised Land. But it bears repeating that when they grew hungry in the desert, most wanted to turn back to Egypt "where at least we had bread." That may have been certain, but it would hardly have given them security.

THE FERTILE SOIL OF STOCKS

Ultimately, to be an investor in stocks, you have to believe that American business has a decent future, as well as business worldwide, and that corporations will continue to increase their profits. If you are as convinced of this as I am, then you'll never panic in a correction.
Peter Lynch—legendary manager of the Magellan Fund

If you are like most people I counsel, you may think it quaint to apply principles from the Bible to investing. Yet economics didn't even exist as a discipline until Adam Smith wrote *The Wealth of Nations* at the time when America was being founded. Before then, economics was a branch of moral philosophy, and I can assure you that investment counseling still has much in common with what we hear from the pulpit.

For instance, after Moses kept the Hebrews from panicking and seeking the certainty of bread in Egypt, he led them on toward the security of the Promised Land. And once the next generation entered it, Moses explained how every person was to *own* a bit of the nation's wealth. But they were also forbidden to earn interest by *lending* money to their neighbors. For the next several thousand years, moral philosophers continued this teaching, and Christianity officially promulgated it until about four hundred years ago when the Protestant Reformers began laying the foundation of the Industrial Revolution, which was financed by primitive banking. Islam still officially forbids the earning of interest. As in Islam today, many Jews and Christians over the centuries figured out ways around the teaching, but that's another story.

It might surprise you that after the savings-and-loan problem, which was essentially caused by our lending to those of any character as long as they promised the most interest, the *Economist* advocated a reconsideration of the concept of forbidding interest. Nevertheless, many of my religious clients still feel that earning interest is moral, while owning stocks and other assets is not. That's unfortunate.

In the modern era, owning stocks has produced 10% returns while bonds have produced 5% and money-market investments have produced 3%. And yet most of my clients say, "That's nice, but I want the certainty of earning interest from bonds and money-market investments anyway." So, of course, year after year they return and ask why they can't achieve the financial promised land.

Most of us build our investment philosophies on the marketing strategies of institutions—like governments, banks, and insurance companies—that want to borrow our money. But John and Peter Lynch, as well as other legendary investors, agree that Moses was on to something when he advocated owning outright rather than lending for interest. They regularly tell investors that owning the world's businesses by buying stocks normally produces better returns than lending to institutions by buying bonds, annuities, and certificates of deposit. Yet most Americans continue to seek certainty. For example, Lynch recently estimated Americans own about $6.5 trillion worth of stocks and about $10 trillion worth of bonds.

It is worth noting that Ibbotson Associates in Chicago produces a widely quoted annual study that updates the returns for stocks, bonds, money markets, and inflation since 1925. This year's study showed that small-company stocks have averaged 12.2% return before taxes over that period. Large-company stocks have averaged 10.2%. Long-term government bonds have averaged 4.8%. Treasury bills have averaged 3.7%. (You can normally assume certificates of deposit will return something between Treasury bonds and bills.) And inflation has averaged 3.1%.

The investment firm of Morgan Stanley recently produced a similar study of the past fifty years, which obviously begins after the Great Depression. It also showed that small-company stocks were the best performing assets during that period, averaging over 14%. The S&P 500 stocks had averaged about 12%. Treasury bonds and bills, benefiting from the high rates of the early eighties, had produced about 6% returns. Still, if you pay taxes, the bills and bonds barely kept you ahead of inflation as it, too, was higher during that period.

Regardless of the time frame, the seemingly small differences in percentages can add up to large differences in money. Interest tables tell us that simply increasing your return from 6% to 8% over the typical forty years most people work will more than double your retirement nest egg. The Ibbotson study graphically illustrates what that means in actual money. It says that had you invested $1 in 1925, you would need $8.35 to keep up with inflation. The Treasury bills would have produced $12.19 before taxes; the bonds $25.86; large-company stocks $810.54 and the small-company stocks $2,842.77. Obviously, if you can earn an extra 2% above the small-company average—as John has done by looking beyond our borders and by astute management—the rewards can be substantial.

Despite the superior performance of stocks, when John shared his "Laws of Successful Investing" a few years ago, fearful Americans still had only one-half as high a percentage of their available assets in them as they did in 1968. (It was about 40% in 1968, 20% in 1990, and is about 33% in early 1996.) While past performance is never a guarantee of future performance, it remains one of the most reliable indicators. Obviously, many of us might find more security by owning wealth all around our world than we would from the certainty offered by interest-paying investments.

Yet like my client who owned the stock in the multinational company, many money managers maintain you can achieve the same degree of security by simply investing in American companies that do a significant share of their business overseas. Others argue that as more countries enter the global marketplace by embracing democratic capitalism, their stock markets will move much as ours, so there's no reason to diversify. These arguments may be why the *Economist* recently commented, "At present, American investors hold only 3% of their total financial assets in foreign securities, compared with 25% for British investors and more than 10% of the financial assets of Germans and Japanese."[2] But I don't believe studies validate these arguments against international investing or the concentrated portfolios they have encouraged. Rather, I suspect those arguments are advanced by managers who have yet to develop the ability to invest in international markets.

In a column titled "Diversity Pays," Mark Hulbert recently wrote in *Forbes*:

> Do it right, and you will reduce, rather than increase, the risk that goes with stock ownership. The right way is to invest only a part of your stock portfolio in foreign stocks, keeping the rest invested in the U.S. How can the addition of riskier foreign stocks end up reducing risk? Because foreign stock markets don't move in lockstep with the New York Stock Exchange.[3]

And a recent *Morningstar* study came to an even more optimistic case for mutual-fund investors:

> To say that world equity markets are moving in lock-step is an overstatement. Opportunities for investors to diversify their portfolios overseas are growing, not dwindling. . . . All in all, while the world may be getting more homogeneous, it's still possible—and worthwhile—to pursue diversity.[4]

THE GOSPEL ACCORDING TO RUSH

Nationalism: One of the effective ways in which the modern man escapes life's ethical problems.

Reinhold Niebuhr

When doing talk shows, I inevitably get a call from someone who asks, "Why should we invest overseas when we've got all these problems here at home?" And it usually seems to come from a fellow conservative who assumes if we're doing something good for those outside our borders, we've got to suffer somehow at home. So I'll quote Rush Limbaugh. He recently interviewed Thomas Flanigan, who watches over about $50 billion for the California State Teachers Retirement System. Limbaugh called Flanigan the "Limbaugh Institute's honorary investment adviser."

During the interview, Flanigan commented, "A very fundamental question has been asked: Is it fiduciarily imprudent not to diversify internationally? The answer is: Yes."

Rush Limbaugh replied: "In other words, should you invest in places other than the United States? The simple fact of the matter is—it's a must. Is it not?"

Flanigan responded, "Correct. Our pension system began investing in international securities about a year ago, and those markets are up more than 20% since then. So, diversification works."[5]

Diversification is essentially built on the spiritual principle of "moderation in all things." Most of us have trouble believing there can be too much of a good thing, especially when it's money. But there can be. Stock markets and real-estate markets of a nation are a little like balloons. You can enjoy them when they're gradually inflated or maintained at the perfect level. But if they're expanded too far too quickly, they can pop. Japan is a perfect example. Rather than investing their excess savings all over the world, as John had been advocating, Japan bid the prices of their stocks, bonds, and real estate up to phenomenal levels. And it was fun—until the balloon began to deflate a few years ago.

It is possible for that pattern to be repeated anywhere in the world. As our economy is again dominating those of other nations, it could attract capital from virtually all Americans and from all over the world, which might blow the balloon up too tightly and increase the risks. Geographic diversification is one very important method of reducing that risk.

There are essentially three methods of achieving geographic diversity: global funds, international funds (sometimes called foreign funds), and regional or country funds. As the name implies, global funds can be invested anywhere in the world. Templeton Growth Fund is an example of how they typically function. Over the past half-century, there have been times when the fund has been over one-half invested here in the United States, as in the early 1990s. There have been other times, such as in the late 1960s, when the fund had almost nothing invested here because our stocks had risen to very speculative heights.

Global funds can be divided further into global stock funds, global bond funds, and unlimited funds. While the first two tend to restrict the assets they can consider, Templeton Growth is an unlimited fund that can invest in a combination of stocks and bonds. It is typically invested in stocks as they tend to be the best-performing asset class. But it was about one-third bonds in the early 1970s when most stocks had been bid up to dangerous levels. If you do not have investments and need broad diversification in one fund—or if you do not care to monitor your investments and make the appropriate changes that investors must make from time to time—an unlimited fund, such as Templeton Growth, Fidelity Asset Manager, or several others, are worth your consideration.

If you already have some stock and bond investments that are primarily domestic, you might consider an international fund similar to the Templeton Foreign Fund. Rather than possibly duplicating your domestic holdings as a global fund might, an international fund would invest only in non-U.S. holdings and balance your current holdings. It is worth noting that even though the U.S. has been a great place to be thus far in the nineties, the Templeton Foreign Fund has actually out-performed the Templeton Growth Fund over the past ten years and yet has typically maintained the same "below-average" risk rating from *Morningstar*.

The third way to diversify internationally is the regional or country funds. These would be similar to the Templeton Developing Markets Trust, which invests primarily in the smaller developing countries of the world, or a fund that invests primarily in one foreign country. Each has advantages and disadvantages. My personal preference is to allow the manager as much flexibility as possible so, at the very least, I prefer funds like the Developing Markets Trust. Also, even a person with as much experience with foreign markets as John advocates that conservative investors might limit their investment in the developing markets to about 10%. If you're a conservative investor, Mark Mobius, who manages the Developing Markets Trust, also suggests that you first invest in global or foreign funds, which are somewhat more stable, and then consider the developing markets funds when you are happy there.

Now let me add a caveat. I don't believe there is any real reason to complicate your life by hiring a lot of consultants or reading a lot of publications and then spreading out among dozens of mutual funds. If you went to a broker or planner who purchased a couple dozen stocks or bonds, you would probably feel very diversified. Why don't we feel the same when a mutual-fund manager spreads our money over *hundreds* of stocks and bonds? We should. As John recently told *Forbes,*

> If you own a fund that can invest without restriction in at least 100 different stocks and bonds worldwide, then one fund is sufficient diversification. Even for very large investors with many millions to invest, nothing is gained by owning more than three such funds. You've already achieved maximum diversification. The whole thing is a matter of common sense, but I suppose that's why it's not common.[6]

A WINNING PHILOSOPHY

One of Wall Street's favorite diversions is to speculate as to who is the greatest money manager of our age. Much like baseball fans debating the home runs, batting averages, and games played of Ruth, Gehrig, Aaron, and Ripken, we investment counselors debate the best years, returns, and durability of renowned money managers.

The *Wall Street Journal* played an inning of our game.[7] Beneath the headline "Who's Number One?" it listed John along with seven other legendary money managers of the twentieth century. Then, along with an excerpt from a new book about the great money manager Warren Buffett, the article said, "A good case can be made for Mr. Buffett." I don't know of anyone on Wall Street who would disagree with that statement, nor with *Forbes'* calling Buffett "living proof that nice guys sometimes do finish first." I doubt John himself would disagree with that. But there are some important lessons to be learned by probing beneath the surface of this story.

Two of the money managers mentioned by the *Wall Street Journal* prospered in the early decades of the century when market conditions were quite different from today's. Three of the modern investors realized high returns by making large, highly leveraged bets for clients with very substantial moneys. And three are pertinent to the typical investor: John Templeton, Warren Buffett, and Peter Lynch of the Fidelity Magellan Fund.

Most of us know that Lynch did incredibly well for the average investor by investing heavily in U.S. stocks during the eighties, a decade favorable for that asset class. We seem less conscious of the '73–'74 decline however. Warren Buffett and John, however, have done quite well during the ups and downs of an entire lifetime. They did it, generally, by avoiding debt. Both are legendary for avoiding the short-term trading mentality that is prevalent on Wall Street, and both invested prudently in responsible businesses that could create wealth for themselves, their shareholders, and our neighbors.

While Buffett's average performance was higher than John's, there was an important distinction. Like Peter Lynch, Buffett invested heavily in the U.S. And U.S. stocks didn't always cooperate during Buffett's lifetime. The *Wall Street Journal* excerpt said Buffett reduced his investing activities in the late sixties yet his remaining portfolio declined "by half" during the decline of 1969 to 1974.

When I researched a chart of the performance of the Templeton Growth Fund for the same period, it showed the value of a $10,000 investment made at the fund's inception increased from $51,632 in 1969 to $78,636 in 1974. In essence, John was able to avoid the decline and still prosper by creating wealth around the world. He did it by avoiding excess and providing money where it was truly needed. I think there are moral and spiritual dimensions underlying that strategy.

On an individual level, the excerpt said that the large decline never bothered Buffett and he simply continued to buy stocks at lower prices. I have no doubt that is true. But I know *very* few investors who have that kind of intestinal fortitude. The vast majority would have sold their stocks after losing much less, sworn never to invest in them again, and would have missed most of the subsequent advance. That reality of human nature is why I believe most investors are well served to diversify globally among the several asset classes. And it's why I'll still make a case for John being number one.

five

THE CREATIVE
USES OF MONEY

GOLDEN RULE:
Money should do far more than simply reproduce itself

Each one should use whatever gift he has received to serve others, faithfully administering God's grace in its various forms.
(1 Peter 4:10)

Remain flexible and open-minded about types of investment. There are times to buy blue chip stocks, cyclical stocks, corporate bonds, convertible bonds, U.S. Treasury investments and so on. And there are times to sit on cash, because sometimes cash enables you to take advantage of investment opportunities. The fact is there is no one kind of investment that is always best.

Sir John M. Templeton

There are more than 7,000 different mutual funds in America today. There are even more individual stocks on the various stock exchanges. I am not sure anyone has even attempted to count the various bonds you can choose from. Add certificate-of-deposit offerings advertised by thousands of banks and you can grow numb considering your investment options.

Yet in spite of all these options, you really only have three choices when investing a few extra dollars:

You can own.

You can lend.

Or you can bet.

I will ignore the last choice, which usually includes the arcane worlds of options and futures, because I am convinced that speculation is good for neither the typical investor nor the world we live in. But the first two can enrich us if we always remember that financial independence is basically an illusion. When we invest, whether we like it or not, we are *always* financially connected to others.

We often forget that when we buy a share of stock, we become part owner of a company producing goods or services for others. When we buy a Treasury bond, we are lending money to the federal government to do something for ourselves and for others. When we buy a municipal bond, we are lending money to a state or local government to do the same thing. And when we buy a certificate of deposit, we are lending money to a specific kind of corporation—called a bank—that will in turn lend our money to others. (You would be surprised how many people tell me they don't trust corporations so they keep their money in the bank!)

For most of this century, as we have seen, owning part of a company has been the most rewarding type of investment, and, although most of us don't think much about it, that is only logical. Companies exist to produce wealth, while governments exist primarily to regulate behavior, secondarily to transfer wealth, and to a lesser extent to create it. Yes, I know some observers say "government never creates wealth." But I believe the creation of national parks and the interstate highways that take us to them are as valuable as many of the amusements created by entertainment companies that reach out to us over the information superhighway.

Banks simply transfer wealth temporarily between depositors and borrowers. So their ability to create wealth depends on whether the borrower obtains a business loan and uses it to produce wealth or obtains a consumer loan and uses it to consume wealth.

It is only logical that your odds of prospering are better if you finance the creation of wealth, rather than its regulation, transfer, or consumption—but as I've said before, that doesn't mean we should keep all our assets in stocks. I reiterate—and emphasize—that for a higher level of personal security, most of us should keep certain percentages of our money in other asset classes.

There are additional reasons to consider other investments as well. As the old saying goes: Growth for growth's sake is the philosophy of the cancer cell. In other words, our economy often creates "wealth" without necessarily enriching American life. Do all music, movie and casino companies really add to American life? Sound money management does far more than simply create more money.

GOVERNMENT BONDS—A DIFFERENT TYPE OF SOIL

Look at the desert from the mountains and you see no life at all. Walk through it, though, and you will find places where life holds its own, even patches where it prospers.

The Economist

During most of the past decade I have owned a few Treasury bonds. Yes, I knew I was financing the deficit spending of our federal government, but unlike those who despised the deficits from the mountaintop of anti-government ideology—but financed them purely out of the down-to-earth desire to protect their personal wealth—I invested in them because I thought our country needed to finance important projects like winning the Cold War.

And yes, I thought I could make more money in stock mutual funds. But my parents and grandparents sacrificed in the short-run, but prospered in the long-run, by buying war bonds. So why couldn't I help our country out a little? I did. And not only did I earn a decent return, I felt better about the future of our nation.

While many Americans operate out of this same kind of "enlightened self-interest," few of us understand the larger financial issues involved. If someone took the time to truly enlighten us about what is happening in our communities, nation, and world, I sincerely believe we would finance certain needs out of positive motivation rather than out of selfishness or fear. That would surely help our world by helping those who are angry about the present and anxious about the future. Let me tell you about an experience I had that demonstrates the rewards of being part of the solution rather than part of the problem.

Just before the elections of 1994, a nationally syndicated talk show asked me to debate a man who had just participated in one of the most pessimistic economic videos I have ever seen. It focused almost entirely on all the things he thought were wrong with our government. About five minutes into the hour-long debate, it became obvious that the only fact he knew about our economy was the size of the federal debt. His thoughts about the debt even prompted one young caller to ask if government bonds were safe investments.

As I began to put the debt into perspective, my opponent invoked images of the Great Depression and asked me how I could possibly condone such "borrowing and speculating." Now, I have never condoned borrowing and speculating so I wasn't sure where his argument was coming from. Later, however, I discovered that the man had spent years speculating in the highly leveraged world of the Chicago commodities pits.

After the debate, it dawned on me that if he had spent more time among the tens of millions of Americans who truly create wealth, he might have been more optimistic about our future. Had he taken the time to look beyond the size of our federal debt to understand something about its nature, he might have been happier to finance some of it rather than let it make him so angry and so certain that America is "doomed." And had he truly analyzed our economy rather than simply criticizing our government, he might have been concerned that his fellow commodities traders around the world now make more short-term bets *each day* on bonds and currencies of greater value than our government spends *in an entire year*. They bet even more on stocks, grain crops, oil, and so on. The value represented by all these bets made at any given time now approximates about *four times* the amount of our federal debt.

Over the years John has simply said all this betting doesn't make enough financial sense to merit his participation. But Peter Lynch has been more vocal in saying all this speculation diverts enormous amounts of money away from small companies that would have used it more productively for research, development, manufacturing, and so on. In a related area, Lynch has pointed out that casino gambling, which produces little real wealth, may soon become the largest industry in our country. Together, his points should give pause to us conservatives who claim, often with moral certainty, that government spending is waste that the private sector would automatically put to more creative uses.

One can only wonder if our young caller would have worried so much about the safety of investing in government bonds had those producing pessimistic economic videos and talk shows shared these statistics. As we investors listen to them, we might remember that psychologists speak of projection—the human penchant of seeing in others what we are afraid to confront in ourselves. It is sort of like gospel singers who sing of faithfulness but have affairs, or those who pile debt on their corporations but worry about the federal debt.

Two Ways of Worshiping

The Heritage Foundation recently released a major study titled "Why Religion Matters: The Impact of Religious Practice on Social Stability." One of its more interesting points is that there are two forms of religion. Building on Matthew 23, it said:

> Recent advances in the investigation of religious behavior have led social scientists to distinguish between two distinct categories of orientations: "intrinsic" and "extrinsic." Intrinsic practice is God-centered and based on beliefs that transcend the person's own existence. Research shows this form of religious practice to be beneficial. Extrinsic practice is self-oriented and characterized by outward observance, not internalized as a guide to behavior or *attitudes*. The evidence suggests this form of religious practice is actually more harmful than no religion: Religion directed toward some end other than God, or the transcendent, typically degenerates into rationalization for the pursuit of other ends such as status, personal security, self-justification, or sociability.
>
> The two orientations lead to two very different sets of psychological effects. For instance, "intrinsics" have a greater sense of responsibility, and greater internal control, are more self-motivated, and do better in their studies. By contrast, "extrinsics" are more likely to be dogmatic, authoritarian, and less responsible, to have less internal control, to be less self-directed, and to do less well in their studies.
>
> Extrinsics are more self-indulgent, indolent, and likely to lack dependability. For example, the most racially prejudiced people turn out to be those who go to church occasionally and those who are extrinsic in their practice of religion.

> In general, intrinsics are less anxious about life's ups and downs, while extrinsics are more anxious. . . . In an ironic set of findings on anxiety about death, extrinsics fared worst of all: worse than intrinsics and worse than those without religious beliefs.
>
> From a purely social standpoint, the intrinsic form of religion is thus good and desirable, and the extrinsic form is harmful.

As individuals, we will be more successful if we don't let such dysfunctions dictate our feelings about the economic future and our investment plans, and as a nation, we will be more successful if we don't let them dictate our public policy.

Psychological well-being aside, there are good reasons to lend to others by owning different types of government bonds. Though John and I might disagree about certain aspects of this, Sherry and I have had a mortgage since we were married. I suppose we could have been better off financially if we had rented until we had saved what we needed to buy a home, but there is something intangible about home ownership that can't be measured financially. And renting isn't always economical either. So we have always lived in a home that cost about one-half of what bankers assured us we could afford with our income, and we have financed them after making substantial down payments. Nevertheless, we have avoided the other forms of consumer debt, so the risk to our lenders has been small. This, as much as our personal financial and spiritual well-being, is what moral philosophers have been interested in throughout history.

One way to enrich yourself as you help those seeking home ownership is through purchasing government bonds called "Ginnie Maes." Most of us know we can obtain a mortgage loan from a financial institution. We know we then make a monthly payment of principal and interest to that institution. But we don't always understand that institutions increasingly sell those mortgages to investors. So the bank takes a small fee for servicing the monthly payment and sends the rest of the principal and interest on to the investors who purchased the mortgage.

Before being sold to investors, some of those mortgages are first insured through a quasi-governmental agency called the Government National Mortgage Association, "Ginnie Mae," for short. The government essentially assures investors that the payments will be made.

That's an important point since those who made the loan would have little way of knowing the people who borrowed their money. Both are increasingly mobile due to the nature of our modern culture.

So, in essence, if you decide to purchase a "Ginnie Mae," you can get a reasonable return that is often close to 1% above Treasury bonds and a monthly check from a government-guaranteed source. In the meantime, you have enabled someone to own a home.

There are some important things to remember about Ginnie Maes and similar bonds, like Fannie Maes or Freddie Macs. Just as you can obtain various types of mortgage loans, you can purchase various types of mortgage bonds. Just as I thought the fifteen-year mortgage made more sense than the thirty-year when we were borrowing, I now think the fifteen-year Ginnie Maes make more sense than the thirty-year variety when I'm investing by lending. The fifteen-year Ginnie Maes are called "Midget Ginnie Maes" and are available through most brokers.

One of the most important things to remember is that each monthly check you receive contains both interest *and principal* payment. So if you spend all your check, you will eventually run out of money. It is primarily for that reason many investors prefer to purchase Ginnie Maes through mutual funds where they typically reinvest the principal and send only the interest payment to you.

Another reason people often prefer mutual funds is the lower minimum investment. Ginnie Maes often cost up to $25,000 each. Mutual funds usually accept a few hundred dollars.

And there may be an even more important reason many people consider mutual funds. As we have discussed, most investors need more growth in the early years of life and more income in later years. Mutual funds can be a convenient way to meet your changing needs and reallocate those funds over a lifetime.

For example, using our asset allocation tip, a young couple aged thirty might place 70% of their money in the Templeton Growth Fund and 30% in a related Franklin U.S. Government Securities Fund, which, by the way, *Morningstar* recently concluded "remains one of the best ways to invest in government bonds."[1] As investors grow older, they can conveniently dial a toll-free number every few years and re-balance their portfolio by increasing the percentage of government bonds they own.

Those who aren't quite as conservative might consider the same concept with a fund like the Franklin Income Fund. In addition to government bonds, the fund may also invest in corporate bonds, utility stocks, and other securities that produce taxable income. Such diversity is most attractive. And it is affordable since the fund accepts $100 deposits. *Morningstar* says Franklin Income has produced about 2.4% more per year on average over the past ten years than the Government Securities Fund has.

Those in a high tax bracket might consider the same approach with a fund like the Franklin Federal Tax-Free Income Fund. *Morningstar* says it is the largest fund investing in municipal bonds from across our country. A quick glance at its holdings indicates it primarily finances utility projects, airports, and health-care facilities. Again, while a portfolio of those bonds might cost tens of thousands of dollars if you purchased them individually, the fund is available to anyone with $100.

Regardless of your temperament and needs, any combination of these Franklin/Templeton funds, or similar funds from other mutual-fund companies, offer the same opportunity for diversification and rebalancing your portfolio every few years.*

A BANK ANY CONSERVATIVE—
OR LIBERAL—COULD LOVE

My friends on the right call for a colorblind society and then quote Martin Luther King's inspirational "I Have A Dream" speech, in which he imagined a nation in which every American would be judged, not on the color of his or her skin, but on the "content of his character." All too often though, they neglect to quote the end of his speech, where he describes the painful plight of minority America: "The Negro," King said, "lives on a lonely island of poverty in the midst of a vast ocean of material prosperity." . . . *The Good Shepherd reminds all of us that our work is not done, and as we think about moving into the 21st century, we must not leave anyone behind.* . . . *Of the 14 million small businesses in existence across the United States today, fewer than 2% are black-owned. And of $27 trillion to $28 trillion of capital in this country, less than 1% is in black ownership.* . . . *Opportunity means the ability to accumulate property.*[2]

Jack Kemp, Empower America

---

* Any broker or financial planner can provide information, or call 1-800-342-5236 for a prospectus. Phone numbers for other fund companies are located farther along in this book.

If you were to ask John about his favorite Bible story, he would probably quote the parable of the talents. Here's how he tells it in *The Templeton Plan*:

> A man going on a trip entrusted his property to his servants. He gave one man five talents [coins worth about $1,000 each], another two, and another one, each according to his abilities. While he was gone, the man with five talents traded with his money and made five talents more. And the man with two talents traded his and made an additional two talents. But the man with one talent buried his master's money in the ground.
>
> When the master returned, he went over his accounts with his three servants. The man entrusted with five talents explained that he'd invested and made five more. And the man given two talents also showed how he'd put his talents to work and now had four talents. The master complimented them both, told them that they had been faithful servants, and that he would entrust them with greater responsibilities.
>
> The man with one talent came forward and said, "Master, I figured you're a hard man and you might rob me of my earnings, so I hid this money in the ground."
>
> His master replied, "You're a wicked and lazy slave. You knew I'd demand your profit. You should have put my money in the bank where it would draw interest. Give your money to the man with ten talents. For to the man who has, will be given more. And from the man who has nothing, even his nothing will be taken away!"

Of course, the original version of that story can be found in Matthew 25. Jesus was the original storyteller, and he was obviously talking about many kinds of talents, not just financial. While I doubt Jesus was interested in investment counseling, there is no reason to believe he sought to exclude our talents as creators of wealth. So I was pleased a few years ago to find a bank that I think Jack Kemp, Sir John Templeton, and even Jesus might approve of.

During the eighties as the savings-and-loan problems were just beginning to surface, I was with a major investment firm that was channeling millions of dollars to the now infamous Charles Keating of Lincoln Savings and Loan. I had never heard of Keating or his activities at the savings and loan. Nor did I have any interest in asking about either. I just knew he was paying my retired clients an extra half percent of interest on their CDs and helping me make a living in the process. Yet I was beginning to hear some things that troubled me. Also, I was just beginning to understand that even the most conservative uses of money can create big headaches.

So I began to shop for a different kind of banking institution for my son's college fund. I heard about one in Chicago called the South Shore Bank. It was founded over twenty years ago by investors, such as the Mennonite Church and the United Church of Christ, who thought banks should help relieve the headaches of a society rather than create them.

At that time, it began gathering deposits from all over the country. It brought them into an inner-city area that both the government and the private sector were rapidly losing faith in. It has since applied the same philosophy to suburban and rural areas. It specialized in financing the rehabilitation and purchase of affordable housing. This did several things. First, it increased our nation's stock of private affordable housing. Second, it created jobs for those rehabilitating the buildings. Third, it helped turn many welfare recipients into taxpayers. Fourth, it allowed them to buy more goods and services, and as a result retailers and service providers began to return to an area they had abandoned years earlier. In essence, the bank breathed life and hope back into dying communities.

When I first heard about the good things South Shore was doing with deposits, I assumed that it was going to cost me somehow. Yet by keeping its overhead low, South Shore pays the same competitive rates as other banks I know of—at least since Charles Keating is no longer transferring taxpayer money to depositors. I get the same government insurance as any other bank, though I doubt I'll ever need it since South Shore's financials remain very solid. In the meantime, I feel more hopeful for the inner cities and rural areas as each quarterly report from the bank tells me I'm making a positive difference in our country. Theologians and ministers should be careful inferring that Sherry and I, as well as other investors, might share the guilt of the "rich young ruler" for that.*

REAL ESTATE—SOLID FOUNDATIONS

The total area of Japan is smaller than the area of Montana, but the market valuation of the real estate is greater than all fifty states of America. . . .

---

*If you'd like to explore both the financial and spiritual rewards of South Shore, call them at 1-800-669-7725. The bank offers certificates of deposit, IRAs, and the other typical banking programs. Note: You should know that I recently began serving as financial adviser to the bank's retirement program and would therefore indirectly benefit in a small financial way if you help the bank expand its work.

Gradually, the Japanese people will send their money out of Japan to buy where the bargains are.

Sir John M. Templeton, *Outstanding Investor Digest*
(February 8, 1990)

Stocks are not the only area of life where excess can be dangerous to the investor's and the nation's well-being. Since John spoke those words about the excesses in Japanese real estate, its value has tumbled some 60%, even more than Japanese stocks. Some analysts fear the decline may even endanger several of Japan's banks.

Of course, to a lesser extent, we in the U.S. have learned the same lesson. While the *Economist* recently said that the real value of our residential housing has been fairly stable since the mid-eighties, our commercial real estate has tumbled about 50% during the same time.[3] Several of our banking institutions have failed because of speculative real-estate loans, and thousands of investors have lost tens of millions in speculative real-estate limited partnerships. Because of those failures, real estate, for several years now, has been one investment most of my clients don't care to discuss.

Still, if you truly understand investing, that fact gets your attention. As an investment counselor, you learn early that if clients are eager to discuss an investment, it is probably the wrong time to invest in it. Remember when everyone *wanted* to talk about real estate? Wrong time to invest. Remember when everyone talked about the oil shortage? Wrong time. Remember when everyone talked about gold going to $3,000 an ounce? Wrong time. So the fact that very few of my clients want to talk about commercial real estate, even though it has dropped by 50% while domestic stocks and bonds have soared to much higher levels, means it is a good time to talk about it. In early 1996, Sir John said it was the only American asset class that really interested him.

Most people don't understand it, but the drop in real-estate prices occurred because we built a lot of *useless* real estate during the seventies and early eighties. In downtown Tampa alone, three huge office buildings stood nearly empty during the early nineties. Many shopping centers proved nearly as useless as the consumer binge slowed. Many of us discovered that owning or financing these properties was a terribly difficult way to prosper.

If you read John Templeton's books or talk with him, you will quickly discover that *useful* is one of his very favorite words. For example, he once told me, "One thing I feel very sure about is that every *useful* work is a ministry, with emphasis on *useful*. Whatever you do that is *useful* to other people, you are doing a ministry. And business is one of the largest ministries on earth because it is the one that helps people to become prosperous." So it might follow that the creation of truly useful real estate might be a rewarding endeavor.

I actually found that was true even during the eighties. Most of my clients thought it was impossible to make money in real estate during that time—but it wasn't if you were careful to pick truly useful real estate. For example, during most of that time, some of my clients diversified a portion of their money into real-estate investment trusts called Corporate Property Associates. They were put together by a man named W. P. Carey. He purchased large buildings from major corporations and leased them back under long-term leases, so he knew the properties were useful to them.

The programs usually began with an 8% income, which was about 50% sheltered from current income taxes because of depreciation on the properties. But the key to the program was that rather than having a "fixed income," like a certificate of deposit or bond, the income from the properties was indexed to rise with the Consumer Price Index. Again, that structure recognized that security is different from certainty.

That recognition served my clients well. Virtually every program increased its dividend over the years as the CPI continued to rise but most "fixed-income" investments paid lower and lower income. Some of the earlier programs have more than doubled their quarterly dividends since the early eighties. And of course, any investment that can steadily create more income is most useful and bound to retain or increase its value. A *Fortune* article titled "How to Get Rich Yield Plus Inflation Protection" quoted an analyst who said, "The W. P. Carey deals have been the best overall during the last ten years. And they're also the only real estate deals that trade at a premium in the secondary market."[4]

A *People* magazine article about Carey suggests that a man with ethics can be a good man to have watching over your money. In essence, it said Carey's grandparents owned a tiny sugar refinery that had gone bankrupt. It was left to Carey to close it down. During the process it bothered him that "the more professional creditors like banks and insurance companies knew how to protect their interests while the poorer farmers had to absorb their losses."[5]

So even though he legally owed them nothing for services they had rendered more than twenty years ago to his grandparents, and received no tax breaks from the IRS as a businessman or philanthropist, Carey sent $250,000 to eighty unsuspecting beet growers because he thought it was the right thing to do.

That is a good story to remember the next time you read one of those too-often-true, but too-often-cynical stories about all the misdirected people who put real-estate deals together during the eighties. Again, being mindful of both our national assets and our national liabilities can make our country and its future look a little better. And I consider W. P. Carey to be one of those assets.*

THE HIGHER BOTTOM LINE

Lives of great men oft remind us
That we can make our lives sublime
And departing, leave behind us
Footprints in the sands of time.
Henry Wadsworth Longfellow

Can you imagine coming up with an idea that would improve the lives of millions and yet believe you shouldn't profit from it? Most of us don't think that way anymore. But Benjamin Franklin did. After he invented the Franklin stove, he refused to patent it on philosophical grounds. He believed, "As we enjoy great advantages from the inventions of others, we should be glad of an opportunity to serve others by any invention of ours."

That kind of thinking springs from the heart and soul. It requires a great deal of faith in the future and a great deal of love of neighbor. And it is most rewarding. How? Do you remember what happened to the money of the richest man of Benjamin Franklin's day? Neither do I. But I do remember that Franklin enriched life for my ancestors as they struggled to create a new nation. As important as financial rewards are, they are rarely legacies of the eternal variety.

---

*The real-estate trusts are offered through several investment firms, but you can obtain a prospectus by calling 1-800-972-2739. Minimum investment is $5,000, or $2,000 for an IRA. As with all real-estate investment trusts, there is a market for the units if you have to sell. But, as with all real-estate investments, you will be well served by holding on to your investment for ten years or longer.

six

THE POWER
OF PATIENCE

GOLDEN RULE:
Remember that patience is a virtue

One eager to get
rich will not go
unpunished.
(Proverbs 28:20)

Invest—don't trade or speculate. The stock market is not a casino, but if you move in and out of stocks every time they move a point or two . . . or if you continually sell short . . . or deal only in options . . . or trade in futures . . . the market will be your casino. And, like most gamblers, you may lose eventually—or frequently.[1]

Sir John M. Templeton

I was once invited to New York to speak to about sixty denominational stewardship leaders from across North America. My subject was the need for theologians to interact with business leaders so we might better convert belief into practice.

To demonstrate that theologians often speak to one another in lofty ideals that often mean little in daily life, I asked if any of them had ever spoken on the virtue of patience. Of course, all of them had. I then asked if any of those who owned mutual funds had any idea if their manager was practicing patient investing or speculating for short-term gain. Not one had any idea or even knew how to find out once I had sparked their curiosity.

THE EYE OF THE STORM

The global currency markets now trade over $1.1 trillion a day. Each week they shift wealth equal to the gross domestic product of the United States. Every five hours they trade the equivalent of this year's U.S. defense budget. Against such financial tsunamis, it is increasingly difficult to argue sensibly that any elected government, American or other, can elaborate and deploy an independent national economic policy.

Martin Walker, *World Policy Journal*

Imagine you go to a local investment firm and ask how the broker plans to invest your money. Suppose he replies that he will trade all your stocks each year on average and your bonds even more quickly. Would you let that broker manage your money? Probably not. Would you consider yourself an investor rather than a trader if you did? Hopefully not.

Yet I just described the trading pattern of the typical mutual-fund manager who watches over our money. Many fund managers have contributed mightily to the development of what one prominent critic has termed, in a book by the same name, *Short-Term America.*[2]

America hasn't always been that way. I began my career on Wall Street in the late seventies with Merrill Lynch. I remember we cheered one day when the New York Stock Exchange traded an incredible 40 million shares of stock. And I can remember going to the office one Saturday to find the order entry personnel busy at work, even though the exchange was closed. They were conducting a test to see if the firm could handle days when the exchange might trade 100 million shares of stock. In a most nonprophetic way, I remember thinking that could never happen.

Now, on average, the exchange traded over 330 million shares each day in 1995. The NASDAQ, which carries shares of smaller companies, trades an even greater number each day. There are two good reasons to understand your fund manager's role in that increased trading: your own good and the good of your country.

For your own good, you should know that mutual funds like to call speculating and trading "portfolio turnover." It is normally expressed as a percentage and can be found in any *Morningstar* report or toward the bottom of the statistical chart found in the first few pages of any fund prospectus.

As an example, if a stock fund manager has traded all his stocks each year on average, the fund would have a portfolio turnover of 100%. If he traded twice a year, it would be 200%. If he traded only every two years on average, it would be 50%. You get the picture. It is not unusual for even some of the best-known fund houses to trade at over 200% annually.

Over the years, I have come to believe that such rapid trading cannot be in your long-term interests. In fact, I am convinced that low portfolio turnover is one of the most important indicators of success.

For example, *Forbes* annually publishes its Honor Roll of mutual funds. These are the funds *Forbes* believes have offered the best risk-adjusted returns over periods approximating the previous decade. In its words, "Short bursts of glory won't get a fund on the *Forbes* Honor Roll. Consistency of performance and toughness in tough times will." I've analyzed the portfolio turnover of the ninety-seven fund listings they have honored from 1991 to 1995. During those five years, they have averaged only 38% turnover—about one-third of the typical mutual fund. Of the ninety-seven listings, only five traded as much as the typical mutual fund. Each one of those five made its appearance on the Honor Roll over three years ago and has not repeated since.

Morningstar has done a broader study that validates my Honor Roll analysis of the top funds. It grouped funds according to low turnover of 50% or less; moderate turnover of 50 to 100%; and high of over 100%. It then analyzed the risk-rewards of all three groups. Its conclusion was:

> As the mutual fund industry has ballooned, so has portfolio turnover. Whereas the average U.S. diversified equity fund took just over two years to divest itself of a typical position in 1977, it now requires barely one year. . . . As portfolio turnover has risen, however, so has the evidence against such a practice. . . . In a nutshell, low-turnover funds have made more money and assumed less risk than have moderate-turnover funds, which in turn boast the same advantages over high-turnover funds.[3]

Watching the trading habits of your fund manager can be terribly important for several reasons. Obviously, the first is that rapid trading can be expensive. In 1987, the most recent year I have statistics for, Americans spent $25 billion trading stock certificates. That was a figure approximately equal to one-sixth of all corporate profits and 40% of all dividends paid out that year.

Yet commissions are highly negotiated for mutual funds. So the cost that is perhaps even more important for mutual-fund investors is known as "slippage." In essence, this means a fund manager who wants to buy $1,000,000 worth of a $10 stock might have to pay up to $10.25 or more to get all he wants. That doesn't sound like much, but the 25-cent difference is 2.5%. And that's just to buy the stock, not sell it at a later time. In the words of a *Barrons'* article,

> As a fund with a good track record becomes large, the cost of entering and exiting positions becomes prohibitive. For example, the slippage in buying and selling 100,000 shares of a $50 stock is roughly $1.50 a share each way, or $300,000 on a $5 million trade, which is 6%.[4]

The *Wall Street Journal* has quoted Gerald Perritt, editor of the *Mutual Fund Letter*, as saying,

> Most of us fund managers are paying anywhere between 4 cents and 8 cents per share (in commissions). But the big thing is the spread. The spread on a round trip, large-block trade is probably between 3% and 6%.[5]

Again, notice that slippage or spread is *in addition to* commission costs, which are a relatively minor concern for funds. And be aware that neither commissions nor slippage expense is included in the annual "expense ratio" that some mutual-fund investors have learned to watch. That ratio only includes legal, accounting, and similar costs that the fund incurs.

Another cost of rapid turnover is taxes. Assume you are considering two funds. Both have track records of returning 10% per year and appear equally rewarding. Yet one trades in the typical fashion and therefore creates 10% gains to be taxed each year. Assuming you are in the 30% tax bracket, you pay 3% to Washington and keep 7% working for you.

But the other fund tends to invest more and holds stocks five years, thereby trading only 20% of its portfolio each year. So despite making the same 10% return, it only realizes 2% to be taxed that year. If you pay 30% taxes on the gains, you send 0.6% to Washington and keep 9.4% working for you. In essence, it is tax deferral with benefits similar to a retirement plan or annuity. In reality, stocks held for more than one year are taxed at a maximum rate of 28% regardless of your tax bracket, another advantage of patience.

The wisest investors understand this very well. The *Morningstar* study added this counsel from Warren Buffett, an outspoken critic of short-term trading who often says his favorite holding period is forever:

> Warren Buffett hardly sold any stock shares during the 1980s, all the while deriding high-turnover buyers. . . . One should remember that these represent *pretax* returns; as Buffett loves to point out, high-turnover investors face even worse real-world results once the government takes its share of their net realized capital gains.

And finally, even mutual-fund managers may need to be in stocks, rather than sitting on cash as they time the market, to enrich us in prudent ways. The Pioneer Funds recently said that over the past sixty years, one of the easiest and safest ways to prosper was to actually be invested! That sounds simple but is ignored by many people, including many fund managers. Pioneer's research said that in any given year, the S&P 500 was up 75% of the time. In any given three-year period, it was up 91% of the time. In any five-year period, it was up 94% of the time. And over any given ten-year period, it was up 100% of the time. A fund manager who jumps in and out of the market has a lot of history going against him.

Mark Hulbert, who makes a living analyzing the claims of market-timing letters, may have summarized it best when he wrote:

> It's tough for an active trader to beat the market when brokerage commissions and bid/ask spreads are counted. Figure in taxes for a high-bracket investor and it's next to impossible. Most active traders are losers. . . . Moral: If you are going to trade actively in a taxable account, be honest with yourself and call it sport, not business.[6]

SOCIAL COSTS

The 1929 breakdown was, at its roots, a moral breakdown. We were not living right. We had become extravagant. We had become intoxicated by the alluring notion that the royal road to riches did not lie through sweat but through speculation. We discarded and scorned old-fashioned virtues.
B. C. Forbes, *Forbes* (April 15, 1932)

It has long been acknowledged that speculation is not only harmful to personal well-being but to the well-being of our nation as well. Michael Jacobs, the author of *Short-Term America*, recently wrote, "There are precious few owners today. . . . When investing in stocks, most of us are pure speculators. . . . The investment industry, among others, would like to keep it that way."

Over the years, I have heard considerable discussion that commission-driven Wall Street advisers encourage investors to trade too often. There is obviously considerable truth in that claim. But it might surprise you that a recent study said those who buy mutual funds without the assistance of brokers—no-load investors in other words—trade their funds about *twice as often* as investors who buy load funds with the assistance of a broker.[7]

All that trading by speculators can even hurt the patient investors who just sit still in a fund. *Forbes* recently said,

> Every net dollar coming in or out of a fund at the end of the day contributes to a trade the next morning, and every trade contributes to a drag on performance. Transactions with shareholders, meanwhile, contribute to the expense ratio.[8]

Two personal stories might help you to better understand that many financial writers encourage a lot of this coming and going from funds—even as they write about the dangers of trading with a commission-driven broker.

In the early nineties, I started a small newsletter to help ethical and religious investors. Month after month, I essentially said the American economy is better than most people think and that readers should buy a small group of prudent and ethical investments, primarily mutual funds, to hold for the long-term. But despite preaching the old Wall Street gospel that investors make more money wearing out the seat of their pants than the soles of their shoes, I would lose readers virtually every month who couldn't understand why they should pay me to advise them to sit still.

So after a while, I realized I didn't have the marketing muscle to reach those true long-term investors who might find my approach helpful. When someone told me I might refer my readers to a much larger newsletter that addressed similar topics for a similar market, I was interested. The editor sent sample copies of past letters.

In one of the first, he had written, "My whole philosophy is to diversify into carefully selected stock and bond funds, and then hold on for the long-term." The following month, he discussed market-timing and quoted John Templeton and Warren Buffett as being opposed to the practice. He concluded, "I've elected to make a diversified buy-and-hold approach the basis for my advice."

Yet a few months later, the Dow had risen through the 3000 level and he wrote:

> I am moving 20% out of stock funds and into interest earning funds. . . . If you are currently dollar-cost-averaging a large amount on a short-term basis, stop investing in the stock funds for now. . . . I would recommend calling a temporary halt while you wait for the market to return to the fair value range. . . . This isn't a "market-timing" step we're taking.

And yet that sure sounds like market-timing. But combining our newsletters still seemed to make sense, so we did. Yet during the next several years, he claimed the market would drop while recommending that our readers should trade their remaining stock funds every few months.

The lesson is that this was all he really could do because of his worldview. Like most publications in recent years, he was pessimistic about the future because of the federal debt and our government. And it is very difficult to tell readers to patiently put a few good funds away for years when you are also telling them earthshaking events are imminent. Despite the fact he *believed* in long-term investing, his perceptions caused him to *act* like a short-term speculator. That is an unfortunate description of most of us these days, for financial success doesn't depend on what we believe but on what we do.

Another lesson to be learned from a parallel scenario was playing itself out in *Forbes* during this same time frame. By now you know I have a great deal of respect for the business information the magazine provides, but in what may have been its worst case of fund-timing ever, its April 15, 1991, edition contained an article titled "Templeton Falls Off the Mountain." It said John had "lost his touch" as a fund manager.

That surprised me. The November 27, 1978, edition of *Forbes* had featured John on the cover. He was caricatured as an owl and the article said:

> One of the hardest things about keeping your head in the stock market, a wise old Wall Street owl once remarked, is that: "You look in the newspaper five days a week, and the quotations tell you how smart or dumb you were yesterday. You get emotionally whipsawed." So it has been this year—with a vengeance. . . . How do you keep your head in a situation like this? What *Forbes* did was make an appointment to see John Templeton, one of the rare birds who can keep his

TEN GOLDEN RULES FOR FINANCIAL SUCCESS

head when the market is doing scary things. He's seen it all or nearly all in his forty years in the investing game. With his cool head and hand, he has produced a spectacular record. . . . *Forbes*, which has interviewed them all, considers John Templeton to be one of the handful of true investment greats in a field crowded with mediocrity and bloated reputations.

The Templeton Growth Fund was a pretty regular member of the *Forbes* Honor Roll for years after that. And in 1991, most of my clients were still as happy with their Templeton funds as investors can be, at least during a global recession.

So it was curious that *Forbes* now seemed to reverse its opinion. So I checked to see if John had deviated from his philosophy of prudence, ethics, and patience. He had not.

John Templeton does not believe he needs to publicly defend himself. He simply has faith that if he does what is right, the truth will become known at the appropriate time. I haven't developed that much faith yet. So I wrote to *Forbes* and said in part, "Bet against Sir John if you want. Not this guy." (To its credit, *Forbes* printed my comment.)

During the remainder of the year, five Templeton funds won performance awards for best in their category. It was quite possibly the best year ever for the Templeton Funds. And by 1993, the Templeton Foreign Fund was back in the top five of the Honor Roll. By 1994, the Templeton Growth Fund had joined it in the top ten. And by January 1995, the fund manager whom *Forbes* claimed had "lost his touch" in 1991 was again gracing the cover of the magazine with advice on "How to Beat the Market."

The lesson is that those who built their portfolios on the ancient foundations of prudence, ethics, and patience, rather than the winds of current opinion, were richly rewarded, both spiritually and financially.

Yet other than *Forbes* emotionally and financially whipsawing its readers, there was something strange happening that reminded me of my newsletter experience. I had noticed that the newsletter editor often wrote about John's philosophies but never recommended actually investing in a Templeton fund. And while the *Forbes* Honor Rolls and cover stories shared how Templeton's patience, prudence, and ethics had produced superb performance, *Forbes* was also steadily suggesting that investors should consider funds other than the Templeton funds they had honored. It even recommended the Templeton Income

Fund, which is solid, but rarely, if ever, mentioned by John as his favorite fund. *Forbes* accomplished that feat by running a "Best Buy" feature along with its Honor Roll feature.

Why do these journals honor some philosophies and funds but recommend others? In other words, why do they say one thing and do another? I think it is a matter of a philosophy that too many financial publications seem to have adopted recently—that of saving investors money in the short-run rather than making them money in the long-run.

TWO MASTERS

Making load versus no-load the paramount selection criteria can be a dangerous oversimplification. . . . A superior manager or a lower expense ratio can easily offset the cost of an up-front sales charge.[9]

Morningstar

Mutual funds are essentially distributed through one of three channels: (1) the brokers who counsel you about fund selection and earn a commission, called a "load"; (2) the planners who counsel you about selecting a "no-load" or no-commission fund and charge you an annual fee for their services; and (3) publications that counsel you about fund selection for a subscription fee, advertising revenues, or both.

Of course, each thinks their approach is far superior to the others.

Stockbrokers naturally feel the personal service they offer is the best approach. They often say things like, "You'll tip a waiter 10% to bring your food. Isn't it worth 4% to guide your life savings through the seven thousand mutual funds available today?" And it seems to make sense. But too often you are served a dish more palatable to your restaurant and waiter than it is to you.

So you turn to "fee-based" advisers who don't earn commissions but promise objectivity by charging an annual fee to channel your money into no-load funds. But you find that means they ignore the load funds that make up one-half of the mutual-fund universe. And you eventually learn those annual fees get tough to swallow year after year.

So you decide to do it yourself by reading the menu of offerings listed in my friend's newsletter. He regularly runs a column about the dangers of stockbrokers who are driven by commissions or about the *Forbes* Honor Roll changing to different funds each year. And he argues that he is objective since he recommends no commission products and accepts no advertising. It seems to make sense. But then you discover that newsletters are usually just one person's opinion; and each month that person has to offer new strategies for dealing with a hostile world—just to keep you interested and subscribing.

So you turn to *Forbes*, whose various writers steadily share stories about the dangers of financial professionals and newsletter writers. They offer differing perspectives of the markets. And again, that seems to make sense, but then you discover that their advice is often contradictory and changes frequently. You wish you could just talk to one of the writers to clarify matters. But the writer is busy with another new idea that might work better next time.

I hear stories like that every day. If you share these frustrations, rest assured you have plenty of company. You are simply suffering from information overload. The way out of this maze of illusions begins by understanding that all advisers fall short from time to time. It is only natural that each person has his or her own point of view and believes it to be the best way to make a living helping investors. Understand that the way these counselors have chosen to be compensated is rarely a solid foundation on which to build your investment philosophy.

I will discuss financial counselors in greater depth in the next chapter, but for now I will tell you why I think so much money finds its way into inferior funds: The newsletter and *Forbes* could praise John's philosophy but recommend that you put money with fund managers of differing philosophies because their philosophy is built on a devotion to *low-cost funds*, which are not necessarily the best funds. For instance, the Templeton Income Fund may earn several percent a year less than the honored Growth and Foreign funds, but it has a slightly lower sales charge. So it appeals to publications that need to convince you they have saved you more than the price of subscribing.

Over the years, my newsletter friend made "no sales charge" an absolute. Therefore, he *totally* ignores the load funds that make up one-half of the mutual-fund universe. That is a strange practice for those promising totally objective advice. You might find it enriching to note that while *Forbes* strongly advocates no-load funds, only about one-third of the funds making the Honor Roll this decade have been no-load.

I will make the case that you will earn more and pay less in the long-run by avoiding simplistic philosophies like these in favor of a philosophy that is built on the virtues of prudence, ethics, and especially patience—whether found in load or no-load form.

A WINNING PHILOSOPHY

What always impresses me is how much better the relaxed, long-term owners of stock do with their portfolios than the traders do with their switching of inventory. The relaxed investor is usually better informed and more understanding of essential values; he is more patient and less emotional; he pays smaller annual capital gains taxes; he does not incur unnecessary brokerage commissions; and he avoids behaving like Cassius by thinking too much.

Lucien O. Hooper

Lucien O. Hooper, the author of the above quotation, is, like Sir John Templeton, a Wall Street legend. I believe his is the philosophy you should look for in a mutual-fund manager. And if you do, that manager should rightly expect your own philosophy to be similar to these words from *Forbes* magazine about Warren Buffett:

> Buffett's disdain for trends, concepts and the slogans so beloved on Wall Street grows in part from a simple realization that neither he nor any other man can see the future. It also grows from his extreme inner self-confidence: He has not the psychological need for the constant wheeling and dealing, buying and selling that afflicts so many successful business and financial people. When he believes in something, he does not require immediate market upticks to confirm his judgment.[10]

Hooper's philosophy might create fund managers who don't trade our investments as often. Buffett's might create fund owners who don't trade their funds as often. Both might also create financial writers who don't feel compelled to use the weathervane as a capitalist tool.

There is substantial evidence that fund managers who have ethics also tend to be prudent and patient. I like the *Morningstar* reports because in addition to providing both short-term and long-term perspectives on return, they also provide insights into risk and portfolio turnover. *Morningstar* rates risk as either low, below-average, average, above-average, or high. They report the portfolio turnover in the standard percentage format. Remembering that past performance is a useful indicator but never a guarantee of future performance, you might find these reports helpful in analyzing the risk, portfolio turnover, and return of those funds that consider ethics.

In the Templeton group of funds, Growth Fund's risk is rated as below-average. Over the past ten years, its portfolio turnover has averaged exactly 20% per year, about one-fifth the trading done by the typical fund. An investment of $10,000 ten years ago would be worth $39,575 today. Foreign Fund's risk is also rated as below-average. Its portfolio turnover has averaged 18% over the past ten years. An investment of $10,000 ten years ago would be worth $50,386 today. They are load funds.

Among the Pioneer group of funds, Pioneer Fund's risk is rated as below-average. Its portfolio turnover has averaged 16% over the past ten years. An investment of $10,000 ten years ago would be worth $30,458 today. Capital Growth Fund's risk is also rated as below-average and its portfolio turnover has averaged 43% over its five-year lifetime. It has averaged almost 19% annual returns since inception. They are load funds.

Among the American group of funds, Washington Mutual's risk is rated as below-average. It too is a steady member of the Forbes Honor Roll. Its portfolio turnover has averaged 15% over the past ten years. An investment of $10,000 ten years ago would have turned into $37,356 today. American Mutual's risk is rated as low. Its portfolio turnover has averaged 21% over the past ten years. An investment of $10,000 ten years ago would be worth $33,696 today. These are also load funds.

The Pax World Fund's risk is rated as below-average. Its portfolio turnover has averaged 45% over the past ten years. An investment of $10,000 ten years ago would be worth $25,991 today. Pax is a balanced fund that invests in both stocks and bonds so both figures are solid. It is a no-load fund.

The Calvert Social Investment Managed Growth Fund is also a balanced fund. Its risk is rated as below-average. Its portfolio turnover has averaged 30% over the past ten years. An investment of $10,000 ten years ago would be worth $26,703 today. It is a load fund.

The Parnassus Fund's risk is rated as above-average. Its portfolio turnover has averaged 25% over the past ten years. An investment of $10,000 ten years ago would be worth $37,075 today. This fund is a low-load fund.

The Domini Social Equity Fund's risk is rated as below-average. An "index" fund, its portfolio turnover has averaged a minuscule 5% over its three-year lifetime. An investment of $10,000 at its inception would be worth $13,732 today. It is a no-load fund.

You can normally expect bond funds to have considerably higher portfolio turnovers than stock funds. They have bonds mature or called away, and bonds are much less expensive to trade than stocks. That doesn't mean you shouldn't watch the turnover. *Morningstar* shares these statistics that suggest prudence, ethics, and patience are a winning philosophy for income investors as well:

The Franklin U.S. Government Securities Fund's risk is rated as below-average. (Yes, like stocks, government bonds do fluctuate in market value until they mature, so plan to hold for the longer term.) *Morningstar* recently made this interesting comment about the fund:

> Investing the old-fashioned way has paid off for this fund. Once upon a time, investors bought bonds and clipped their coupons for income until the bonds matured. In recent years however, this simple practice has fallen by the wayside—especially among fund managers, who often trade in and out of holdings to bet on interest rates or take advantage of other total-return philosophies. Franklin's philosophy, in contrast, harkens back to the old style: In essence, management simply buys current-coupon GNMAs and clips their coupons until they mature. As a result, the fund's turnover is among the lowest in the group. Ironically, despite their attempts to add value, most peers have not been able to match this fund's record.

Franklin also makes no use of the derivatives that have hurt many funds in recent years. Senior portfolio manager John B. Pinkham once explained their philosophy this way:

> When derivatives first came into the marketplace, we just decided on a policy basis that we wouldn't buy derivatives because it was difficult to gauge the risk involved. Without being able to describe the risk, we couldn't really put them in the portfolios. And we don't want to put stuff in the portfolio that our shareholders don't understand.[11]

The Franklin Income Fund's risk is rated as below-average. Its portfolio turnover has averaged just 21% over the past ten years, a very low rate for a fund invested primarily in bonds. An investment of $10,000 ten years ago would be worth $30,452 today.

The Franklin Federal Tax-Free Income Fund's risk is rated as below-average. Its portfolio turnover has averaged just 32% over the past ten years, very low for a municipal bond fund. As trading creates taxable capital gains even in a municipal fund, *Morningstar* added that the fund manager likes to "hold its bonds for the long term ... giving it nearly perfect tax efficiency." An investment of $10,000 ten years ago would be worth $23,402 today. *Morningstar* rates that "above-average" returns for a tax-free fund.

WHERE TO? HOW FAST?

The only way to avoid mistakes is not to invest—which is the biggest mistake of all. The big difference between those who are successful and those who are not is that successful people learn from their mistakes and the mistakes of others.

Sir John M. Templeton

I accompanied my wife, Sherry, to the beach one day. I began to notice how the people there reminded me of investors making their journeys to financial success.

Most of us were just sitting on the beach, appearing to be peaceful and content. But we weren't going anywhere . . . at least until we had to brave the traffic at the end of the day. We were sort of like CD investors. We thought we had avoided the risks of our environment by not wading in. But inflation can burn like the Florida sun. And retirement can be like a bad traffic jam at the end of the day.

Occasionally, someone who wasn't all that knowledgeable about the gulf waters would spot the fin of a porpoise and yell "Shark!" Well-intentioned, they still scared a lot of people. They reminded me of those trained in politics, journalism, and ministry who see some very natural movements in the economy and interpret them as threats to life as we know it.

Some of us wandered into the shallow water from time to time. We timidly watched the water for predators but felt relatively safe. But it wasn't long until we wandered back onto the sand. We seemed like those CD investors who buy bond funds each time the interest rate tide goes out, only to scamper back on shore each time the tide swamps the bond funds again.

Some of the younger people were on surfboards trying to catch a wave. By the time they had climbed on board, it had peaked and was ready to crash into the shoreline. They excitedly looked for a new wave and repeated the process time and again. But despite expending all that energy, they too went nowhere. They reminded me of most speculators.

Some of the boomer generation had purchased high-powered boats that could generate quick bursts of speed. They had a lot of fun, spent a lot of money on fuel, bounced around a lot and came back to the dock at the end of the day—assuming the boat hadn't broken down first. They seemed like those who subscribe to newsletters and magazines that tell people about the hottest mutual funds.

And some of the more experienced types skippered their own yachts. Years of weathering storms, tides, and channels had given some of them the ability to sail safely out on their own. Yet a few days of gentle breezes had only made others smug enough to run upon the shoals when the wind picked up. They reminded me of the investors at the local discount firms and no-load funds.

But out on the horizon sailed a great cruise ship. Though there would be occasional storms to weather, it had taken them in stride over the years. The captain drew upon years of training and experience to provide a pleasant voyage. And the passengers were bound for distant, interesting places. They reminded me of those who had invested in a solid fund forty years ago and stayed on board each time someone not quite as experienced as the captain had advised them to abandon ship.

How will you spend your days in the sun?

seven

WHOM CAN YOU TRUST?

GOLDEN RULE:
If you want to prosper, investigate before you invest

Whoever loves discipline loves knowledge, but he who hates correction is stupid. . . . The way of a fool seems right to him, but a wise man listens to advice.

(*Proverbs 12:1, 15*)

Do your homework or hire wise experts to help you. People will tell you: Investigate before you invest. Listen to them.

Sir John M. Templeton

Today, as Mark Holowesko manages the Templeton Growth Fund each day, he oversees billions of dollars invested in hundreds of stocks and bonds by tens of thousands of shareholders. Though successful now, the Growth Fund's origins were quite humble. It was founded in Canada in 1954—the first of the Templeton Group of funds. For years, it contained only a few million dollars from the clients of John Templeton's investment firm.

In 1964, when John moved from New York City to the Bahamas, he continued to manage the fund out of a tiny office near his home on the west tip of the island—an office located above the offices of the local police department. Mark Holowesko tells me that when he first joined John, four people worked together in that one small room.

John refused to buy notepads back then. He would staple used copier paper together instead, since he had calculated that savings at about a penny a pad. He knew those pennies ultimately come from shareholders and could be better used for research and other uses. John always flew coach class—and gave the savings to charity. Holowesko remembers that the only time he ever saw John Templeton really angry was when his staff surprised him by reupholstering his old chair, which until then had been held together with Scotch tape.

As a business, the Templeton funds achieved significant success from such modest beginnings in a relatively short period of time. Two of the keys were John's humility and discipline. Another was his relationships with some extremely talented and dedicated people.

THE VIRTUE OF PERSISTENCE

I saved and invested money and positioned myself to seize an opportunity. Everyone has at least one opportunity and through proper positioning he or she can seize the chance to effect success.

John W. Galbraith

After twenty years of outstanding returns in the Growth Fund, John Galbraith suggested to John that together they might make the fund available to even more investors. That was in 1974 when the fund contained a grand total of $13,000,000. To put that into perspective, most experts believe a fund needs about $50,000,000 in assets just to break even for the manager. Just as John has become a legend in mutual-fund management, Mr. Galbraith is now a legend in mutual-fund distribution. The *Dalbar* mutual-fund service has said, "John Wm. Galbraith's mild manner and gentle disposition defies the true character of the man. His convictions are strong and unwavering and his focus remains constant as is exhibited by the extent of his success."

When John asked Galbraith how much he thought people might invest in the fund, Galbraith simply replied he hoped enough so that he could make a modest living by distributing it. So Mr. Galbraith brought the Growth fund's philosophy and track record to the attention of brokers and their clients. Since, at the time, most people knew little about mutual-fund investing, much less about international investing, Galbraith was only able to acquire $240,000 for the fund the first year. That didn't even pay his expenses. The second was little better, but the third year, finally, showed a modest profit. So, for the first time in three years, Galbraith paid himself a salary.

Then, in 1978, Galbraith moved the fund distributor and its entire staff of one to a tiny office in St. Petersburg, Florida (until only recently, Mrs. Galbraith accompanied him to the office every day and took calls from investors).

Many other wise and dedicated people contributed to the various parts of Templeton's organization in its journey to success. When it merged with Franklin in 1992, the Templeton organization had grown to over a thousand employees, mostly located in the United States. In addition, thirty-two securities analysts around the world research opportunities for shareholders and provide daily counsel to the Templeton portfolio managers who now watch over more than $50 billion within a Franklin/Templeton complex that stewards over $120 billion.

The moral of this small history lesson is this: John Templeton may be a unique individual, but he understands the contributions gifted and dedicated people make to sound thinking and true success. Even today, he takes pains to surround himself with gifted people. It may not be popular in our age of individualism, when so many financial writers and investment services encourage even the most inexperienced investors to fly solo, but John's approach reflects the wisdom of Solomon that "there's strength in many counselors."

Financial experts can be useful to you in one of two ways: indirectly through their many publications and services, and directly through personal counsel.

Looking for the Good in Our Neighbors

An ancient story tells of two men traveling to a distant city. The first approaches the city's gate where he meets the town sage. The traveler asks, "What kind of people live here?" In Socratic fashion, the sage asks, "What kind of people live in your city?" The traveler replies, "The people there are bad-tempered and selfish." To which the sage replies, "You will find the same kind of people here."

The second traveler approaches and asks the sage, "What kind of people live here?" The sage asks again, "What kind of people live in your town?" The traveler replies, "The people there are kind and generous." And the sage replies, "You will find the same kind of people here."

The point is that we usually find what we look for in people, as well as in life. That makes a major survey published by the *Washington Post* in early 1996 worth reflection. The survey was conducted by the *Post*, Harvard University, and the Kaiser Family Foundation. Its major finding was that

> America is becoming a nation of suspicious strangers, and this mistrust of each other is a major reason Americans have lost confidence in the federal government and virtually every other major national institution. Every generation that has come of age since the 1950s has been more mistrusting of human nature, a transformation in the national outlook that has deeply corroded the nation's social and political life.

It went on to detail that those who most mistrust people also most mistrust the government. And they naturally tune it out. Consequently, two-thirds of those interviewed could not name their representative in Congress and half didn't know their representative's party affiliation. And they didn't usually know that government employment and budget deficits have been declining, rather than increasing. This group was naturally more pessimistic about the future than those who did know such facts.

It might therefore profit us to reflect on these words from *The Templeton Plan:*

> God is the source of all love, and if we open ourselves to receive his love, then we are able to radiate it to other people every day. Ninety-nine percent of the people you meet have good motives and mean well. But you must be sufficiently imaginative and sympathetic to see through a crust of self-consciousness and fear to the inner person. There is goodness there waiting to be released.

SOME HELPFUL PUBLICATIONS

The moving motive in establishing Forbes Magazine, *in 1917, was ardent desire to promulgate humaneness in business, then woefully lack-*

*ing. Too many individual and corporate employers were merely mercenarily
minded, obsessed only with determination to roll up short-term profits
regardless of the suicidal consequences of their shortsighted conduct. They
were without consciousness of their civic, social and patriotic duties.*

B. C. Forbes

A week seldom goes by without my dropping by our local grocery
store. The first things I always notice are the financial magazines, the
covers of which are splashed with such claims as "Twenty Ways to Make
20% with Complete Safety." (Keep in mind that John has averaged
slightly less than 15% over his entire remarkable career, which makes
me wonder why John didn't just stop by the grocery store!)

I wish that making money was as simple as many journalists seem
to think. Still, among the many financial magazines, some publications
are more reliable than others, and they can be a great help to you—*if*
you know how to use them.

Forbes

By now you probably realize that I read *Forbes* almost religiously.
Its many writers and columnists provide valuable information and
insights that the independent thinker will find most useful, though, for
that same reason, the inexperienced investor might find the investment
advice contradictory and the views changing too rapidly.

Increasingly, *Forbes* has become quite political—and very conservative—and it is more entertaining than many business publications.
I'm not sure whether those qualities are good or bad, but I still read it.
One business leader I know recently described it as "a *People* magazine
for the business set"—but he reads it anyway. And there are times *Forbes*
seems to deny the social consciousness of its founder. Yet it remains a
fount of information.*

The Economist

If you would like to read about the world's economies through an
economic prism, with fewer of our political and cultural distortions, you
might find the *Economist*, published in England, to be valuable. Though
it offers virtually no investment advice and contains considerable

---

*You can subscribe to *Forbes* by calling 1-800-888-9896. The current subscription rate is $57 a year.

information the typical person doesn't need, the simple charts always found in the back pages are invaluable for seeing beyond the smoke of American economic and political life. They usually detail America's relative income, taxes, deficits, and so on. At the very least, stop by a library once a month and scan the American Survey in the front and the charts in the back pages.*

Worth

Worth is associated with the Fidelity Mutual Funds, but is fairly objective. It features in-depth articles that often challenge conventional wisdom. It also offers broad statistics of the markets and economy, as well as help on personal financial matters.†

The Wall Street Journal

Of course, the *Wall Street Journal* is a must for any serious investor. Its articles provide interesting insight into rapidly changing American life, though its performance charts are often short-term in nature. If taken too seriously, these articles and charts might encourage you week by week into trading virtually any investment you own. Still, I enjoy the editorial pages immensely. They are a treasure of the American state of mind concerning politics, business, culture, and religion. The editorial pages inside the first section are conservative and the back page is more moderate in tone. Liberals will find much to argue with.‡

Morningstar

Morningstar is most useful for the serious mutual-fund investor. It provides a wealth of information, but I would be careful not to pay too much attention to its famous star rankings (one star being the lowest, and five stars the highest). They change often and, frankly, can whipsaw true investors. Mark Hulbert has written, "The average *Morningstar* five-star fund retains that rating for about eight months."[1]

For example, in January 1995, twelve of the five-star funds were international funds. But nine months later, after our stock market soared past international markets during the first few months of the year, there

---

*To subscribe to the *Economist*, call 1-800-456-6086. It currently costs $125 a year.

†Call 1-800-777-1851 to subscribe to *Worth*. It costs about $15 per year.

‡Call 1-800-568-7625. The *Wall Street Journal*'s current rate is $164 per year.

were no five-star international funds. Of course, if you simply followed the star rankings, you would have done the exact opposite of what you should have. You would have been in international funds as the U.S. stock market began its advance but then would have moved to domestic funds as American stocks became expensive.

The stars can also encourage you to ignore some good opportunities. I keep a copy of the November 26, 1993, edition in my files, for it shows that the ten best-performing funds year-to-date were all *one-star* rated funds. They averaged 96.47% returns during the first eleven months of the year.

Those cautions aside, however, *Morningstar* remains the most useful service I have ever used, and I wouldn't buy a mutual fund without consulting it. Other than information about risk, portfolio turnover, ethics, and performance, you might check these facts from *Morningstar before* investing in a fund: their "beta" tool is helpful in that it estimates how much a fund fluctuates. A beta above 1.00 means it fluctuates more than the stock market in general. A beta below 1.00 means it fluctuates less. Conservative investors might look for funds with low betas but solid, long-term performance. That usually means the manager does a good job of protecting your money during market declines—which I believe is a secret to John's success.

Assume you have $10,000 to invest and are considering two funds. Fund A has a history of gaining 100% one year and dropping 50% the second. Fund B tends to gain 10% one year but stays even the next. It sounds strange, but if history repeats, you would be better off in fund B. Take a minute to think about it. Imagine that in fund A your $10,000 doubles to $20,000 the first year. If it loses 50% the second year, then it is back to $10,000. In fund B, your $10,000 gains 10%, bringing the total to $11,000. If it stays even the next year, it is $1,000 ahead of the more volatile fund A. Yet fund A probably attracted lots of money by making the short-term performance charts the first year, just before it collapsed the second year.

The moral is: conservative investors might buy a good fund with three, four, or five stars, a solid performance over ten to fifteen years, and a low beta, then ignore the short-term changes.

Morningstar's "R-squared" tool may be even more useful. It basically tells you how much of your fund's performance can be explained by the movement of our markets. This indicator is useful if you are trying to diversify away some risk. You would be surprised how many investors come to see me and think they have diversified simply because they have five or six good funds, but each one is essentially a mirror image of the other. So when one market corrects, they all correct together.

That is like having a four-wheeled jeep with all four wheels connected to the same shock absorber. What you really want are funds that are like wheels that move independently. No one can make the road perfectly smooth. (John says he has looked for someone to predict the potholes for the past fifty years and has yet to find him or her.) But R-squared can at least help you construct a portfolio with wheels that move independently. Then your financial journey will be as smooth as possible.

Morningstar helps you do that by providing the R-squared for each fund it covers. For example, the R-squared of Templeton Growth fund is currently .87, a little less than the general stock market. But Templeton Foreign is only .27 and Developing Markets is a minuscule .06. So while the Growth Fund may act somewhat like our stock market, at least when it is as heavily invested in the United States as it was in the first half of the nineties, Foreign and Developing Markets will probably act quite differently.

Morningstar also provides insight into whether funds are managed according to the "value" school of investing or the "growth" school. In essence, value investing looks for stocks of mature companies that are inexpensive in relation to earnings, dividends, book values, cash holdings, and other fundamentals. Growth investors are willing to pay more for younger companies that are expanding their businesses more quickly.

I am more comfortable with value investing as it tends to be more conservative. But there are times when traditional growth stocks are out of favor with the public and can be good values. While some counselors believe you should consider both approaches, John has long been considered a classic value investor. I think that is worth noting.*

Value Line

Value Line is a superb service for investors who like individual stocks. I have used it extensively. But as with the *Morningstar* ratings, Mark Hulbert has noted its top rankings only remain that way for "less than six

---

*You can subscribe to *Morningstar* by calling 1-800-876-5005. An annual subscription is $395, or try an inexpensive trial subscription.

months."[2] So be careful paying too much attention to these rankings if you are a true investor.

In fact, in my first book, *The Christian's Guide to Wise Investing*, I suggested buying those *quality* stocks that are rated as *untimely*, a reflection of my belief in what is often called the "contrarian" philosophy. That too is a core belief of Sir John Templeton, though he calls it an "accommodating" philosophy. The basic principle is to watch what everyone is doing, and do the opposite. As John says, "If everyone is so despondent they want to sell their stocks, be accommodating and buy them. If everyone is so greedy they want to buy stocks, be accommodating and sell to them." Whether contrary or accommodating, it is totally against human nature, but it is critical for investment success. And that makes it another area that benefits from spiritual maturity.*

Newsletters

There are dozens of financial and investment newsletters on the market, though I have yet to find one that is especially useful for someone who wants to look on the bright side and simply put a few good investments away for a few years. Most newsletters operate with too many pressures to provide new ideas that will move you to new and different decisions each month. That doesn't mean some aren't useful to those with shorter time horizons. But before you respond to the typically inflated advertising concerning their results, you might reflect on what I call the "20% rule," which says newsletters are like mutual funds and financial counselors: only about 20% of them will ever make you more money than they cost.**

The Bible

Finally, yes, I also encourage you to read the Holy Scriptures. Aside from the broad, abiding truths to be found in every book, I especially love Proverbs and Ecclesiastes because they provide much wisdom.

---

*You can subscribe to *Value Line* by calling 1-800-833-0046. It is $525 per year, but usually offers a trial for $55.

**A major ministry has very recently asked me to consider co-publishing a newsletter devoted to the philosphies found in this book. It appears likely that we may do so. If you would like a sample newsletter, simply send your name and address to me: Gary Moore, P.O. Box 18656, Sarasota, FL 34276-1185.

They were written, you might say, by a wealthy investor and political philosopher of the time—Solomon.

For practical advice, you might also want to delve into Deuteronomy, chapters 27 and 28, for they are filled with great wisdom concerning political economy and personal financial management. It is reported that reformer John Calvin preached more than two hundred sermons based on those two books alone.

Nor was Calvin alone. Even Adam Smith, who is considered the father of modern economics, studied the words of Solomon and Moses for he was, by training, not an economist at all (for the field hardly even existed at that point in history) but a professor of "moral philosophy." Before publishing his seminal book *The Wealth of Nations*, he had written another important book, *A Theory of Moral Sentiments*, which attempts, in part, to bring social and political action into accord with Biblical concepts.

But even more important than the practical wisdom contained in the Bible is the perspective it gives concerning the Way, out of the cave, the Truth, rather than illusions, and the Life of enlightenment rather than darkness. Back in the mid-eighties, when I was deeply confused about the economy and the chaos of Wall Street, I took some time off and retreated to a Kentucky mountaintop to read the Bible. It was an experience that changed me heart, soul, mind. It was one of the few chapters of my life to be punctuated with tears, but it helped to transform the greatest tension I had ever known into the greatest peace. I could go on describing more examples of its benefits, but the Bible, unlike the other written material referred to above, must be experienced by each person in the silence of his or her own soul. My hope is that it might give you the same peace it gave me.

PERSONAL COUNSEL

Morningstar isn't out to tar financial planners; while we recognize that many investors don't need such assistance, we believe that many more need help than know it.

Morningstar

As the nineties began, I decided to leave the investment firm I worked for. I thereby became another American to be "downsized" from the Fortune 500. And though I am making less money, I am actually much happier. Chasing big bucks on the corporate treadmill was no longer my idea of fun. I wanted to establish a small practice that would help true investors, concerned with both prudence and ethics in their financial dealings, find money managers who could meet their needs. Improved technology made this freedom possible. So while many pundits demonize technology for down-sizing, I've chosen to view it as another blessing and make it work for me. While this had the pleasant effect of involving me with some wonderful people, it also gave me the opportunity to evaluate the fairest possible arrangements among clients, counselors, and money managers. If you think there are *any* such arrangements that eliminate all conflicts of interest, rather than merely minimizing and managing them, you probably need to think again.

As a former commission-based broker of many years, I was familiar with the temptations inherent in that approach, so I looked hard at the new annual-fee approaches that are spreading quickly. One such approach is the "fee-based" approach in which you, the investor, pay the counselor a fee to evaluate your situation and then perhaps a commission to purchase an investment for you. As most investors have become too sophisticated to pay twice for counsel, at least when it's properly disclosed, that approach left something to be desired.

The more legitimate arrangement appeared to be the "fee-only" approach, in which you pay once for the counselor to evaluate your situation and then pay an annual fee for the counselor to watch over investments in no-commission products. That annual fee is typically between 1% to 1.5% of your assets, but I recently ran across a widow paying almost 3% annually at a bank trust department. She was getting some basic bill-paying services but mostly oversight for her mutual funds.

There are other serpents in that "fee-only" garden as well. I discovered one, for instance, after I had written my first book that told investors to buy good investments and resist the temptations to trade them. Obviously, if a client followed my advice and held a mutual fund for five to ten years, he or she might pay annual fees that amounted to several times the 2% or 3% initial commissions I had received when utilizing funds like Templeton. (Templeton's sales charge scales from 3.50% at the $100,000 most fee-based advisers require as a minimum to no sales charge at $1,000,000. That makes its funds compare quite favorably with annual-fee services for church retirement plans, foundations, and other larger accounts. If you happen to have over $1,000,000 to invest, the Templeton funds are often less expensive than many no-load funds, yet you still get the advice of a personal broker or planner.) Small wonder Wall Street firms that used to challenge the wisdom of annual fees are now moving quickly in that direction. Even the Templeton funds have recently started an annual-fee arrangement. If you intend to be a long-term investor of five years or more, I question whether these annual fee structures are in your best interests.

There is a more significant problem, however. The appeal of a fee-only practice was its alleged objectivity. Yet as I spoke with its practitioners, I noticed no one ever charged a fee and then suggested clients should pay a commission to enter funds like Templeton. They more often justified the annual fee by explaining they had saved the commission by using no-load funds. But that meant they categorically rejected one-half of the mutual-fund universe, a strange practice when you're charging higher fees but promising total objectivity.

As I was contemplating all this, *Morningstar* devoted an entire article to the subject. It had been invited to structure a portfolio for a national investment challenge, but unlike the other participants, it included some load funds in its portfolio. Its August 10, 1990, edition explained why:

> We felt it was important to pick the best possible funds, either load or no-load, and to make the point that for investors with long-term time horizons a sales charge should not necessarily be a front-line consideration. When amortized over a fifteen year period, the effect of a sales charge is minor in comparison to the effect of managerial ability.
>
> Many fund-industry commentators continue to make dogmatic proclamations that investors should only buy no-load funds. While we agree that no-load funds are better options for some investors, the conclusion that they are the proper medium for all investors is misguided. Such thinking eliminates a number of superb portfolio managers such as Templeton's John Templeton.... True investment talent is a rare commodity. To start one's mutual fund search by eliminating many top managers is hardly a promising course of action. To look just at sales fees, or even to weigh them too greatly, distorts the evaluation procedure and can lead to poor conclusions. Should investors have neglected Fidelity Magellan due to its 3% front-end load?
>
> If one wants to research the mutual fund arena fully, obtain prospectuses and applications, and assemble and monitor one's portfolio, then there is little reason to pay someone else to do these things. That's a

personal choice that all investors are free to make. Unfortunately, the attitude that investors who choose not to do these things are somehow inferior to those who do has been on the rise in recent years.

It's also important to recognize, however, that many of the most vocal critics of load funds and their sellers are in direct competition with planners for an investor's dollars. Book writers, newsletter editors, and financial magazines want individuals to spend money on their publications rather than pay it to a broker. . . . While the initial cost may indeed be substantially lower than a front-end load, the ongoing subscription cost plus the time and energy output required to master the materials could easily outpace the sales charge.

I reflected on that thinking and realized I was about to become one of those counselors who dogmatically rejected funds like Templeton Growth, Washington Mutual, Pioneer Capital Growth, and other fine funds. That didn't seem entirely compatible with an objective and ethical practice. So I stayed with the commission-based system and have gravitated to a commission or annual-fee system as some of the newer no-load funds with an ethic have developed acceptable track records. I would therefore make these suggestions:

First, you should really know yourself. *Honestly* determine whether you need counsel or not. If you can resist all the temptations to avoid investing or to trade excessively and know how tools like international diversification, asset allocation, portfolio turnover, beta and R-squared might be helpful, you obviously don't need a counselor. (If your counselor doesn't know, you may need a new counselor rather than a do-it-yourself approach.)

Second, *honestly* determine if you are capable of making a long-term commitment. If you are anxiety prone, need counsel, and make frequent changes in your portfolio, you are a prime candidate for fee-based counselors. It is an expensive approach, but it is even more ludicrous to pay an initial sales charge every year or two if you move around as often as many investors do.

If you need counsel and can hold investments for five or more years, you should consider a commission-based adviser. If the adviser seeks to channel you into funds his company sponsors—called proprietary funds—and they don't measure up in services like *Forbes* or *Morningstar*, find a new adviser. If an adviser provides constant reasons to change your funds, find a new adviser. And remember, in twenty years,

I have never met anyone who liked paying the commission to buy a fund like Templeton Growth or Washington Mutual—but I have also never met anyone who wasn't glad they did ten years later.

Finally—and, I hope, in a spirit of brotherhood rather than self-service—I offer this suggestion on behalf of the many financial counselors of the world. True professionals understand that there are many ways for you to research and develop your own investment plans. There will be more as technology makes information even more available. But while our initial exploratory sessions with potential clients are normally complimentary and without obligation, we must take care when people take our time and expertise with no intention of establishing a business relationship. As I hope you know by now, some of us invest large amounts of time and money in researching the financial world and its opportunities. Our time and wisdom are all we have to sell to support our families, charities, and so on.

Yet in recent years, callers increasingly tell me that all the financial information around them has totally confused them. Then they tell me the same sources confusing them suggest that they never pay a counselor to straighten it all out. That can be painful. It is especially painful when some of those callers are referred by ministries that preach the same philosophy.

In a larger context, more and more of our neighbors make their livings by providing services and information. Many of us, who would never take apples from a farm or a jacket from a store without paying for them think nothing of asking for information without asking the price or offering any payment. Perhaps we need to update our understanding of the gospel for the times in which we live. It just might be the kind of investment this old world needs.

eight

INVESTING FOR GOOD

> GOLDEN RULE:
> *Never forget: The secret of creating
> riches for oneself is to create them for others*

Unlike Midas, whose wealth exerted a negative force, Templeton had a positive solution to the "problem" of money; he would use his material gains in a way that would benefit others. His attitude toward his worldly success involved a sense of stewardship, a belief that what you have is not actually yours but is held in trust for the good of all humanity.

The Templeton Plan

I was one of the few investment counselors in America totally unconcerned by the stock market crash of October 1987. No, I had not discovered a magic formula, as so many counselors claim to have done, that could protect me from the uncertainties of our world. And no, John Templeton had not taught me how to possess some internal peace that could transcend the thorns and crosses of life.

I was unconcerned about the crash because I was unaware that it had happened. Sherry and I were on an airplane high above the Atlantic, on a return flight from Europe. I didn't learn of the news until after we landed and I called my secretary before catching a connecting flight. She was crying so hard she could barely tell me what had happened. Some of my associates in the office felt a similar despair. Yet that day probably taught me more about life and investing than any of the days to follow—days that saw the stock market resume its trend toward record levels.

As Sherry and I flew home in the still twilight of the jet, the main thing on our minds was how our young son, who was staying with his grandmother, was doing. Nevertheless, news of the crash was the first time in over a decade together that Sherry and I truly began to deal with the uncertainties of the future.

I asked Sherry, "What will we do if things fall apart tomorrow?"

She thought for a few seconds and said, "Why don't we find a small hut on the beach, catch some fish, make a modest living, and watch our son grow up?" Sherry has always retreated to the solitude of the beach when things become troubled.

I thought about that for several minutes. Then I asked, "If things *don't* fall apart tomorrow—if we prosper and can afford to do anything we'd like to—what should we do?"

Without hesitation, she replied, "Why don't we find a small hut on the beach, catch some fish, make a modest living, and watch our son grow up?"

It was then I began to appreciate how much we humans think we want but how very little we really need to be happy. That moment was the beginning of a deepening quest for the truth about material and spiritual well-being. (It might interest you that studies indicate that since 1960 our real personal income has more than doubled, but the percentage of us who say that we are "very happy" has been stuck at 30% since that time.)

A few days later, Louis Rukeyser canceled his scheduled guest and asked John Templeton and Peter Lynch to join him on *Wall Street Week* to explain what had happened. John simply said that these things happen in life, and we should just consider it a unique opportunity to purchase stocks at more favorable prices.

That was a difficult concept to grasp at the time. Stocks are the only thing I know of that most people find harder to buy as they become less expensive. And they had just gotten a lot less expensive very quickly. Yet while others felt despair, John felt eager to purchase stocks for his shareholders at bargain levels. It is all in how you look at your world and the future.

It seemed so simple at the time, but also radical. I have gradually adopted his strategy and have benefited both spiritually and financially. And though Sherry and I didn't move to the beach, I did move my practice into my home so I could simplify my life and watch my son grow up.

Much later I ordered a book by James Ellison, *The Templeton Plan: 21 Steps to Personal Success and Real Happiness*. It was, essentially, Sir John Templeton's personal philosophy of life. Though it contained almost no investment advice, it has paid greater dividends than virtually any investment I have ever made. As Mark Holowesko often says, one of the most important things about John is that "his real genius is simplicity."

When I ordered that book, all I knew about John Templeton was that he had made a higher investment return for investors than any mutual-fund manager since I was born. During the 1980s, that was about all I needed to know to respect the man a great deal. So you can imagine my surprise when I discovered John didn't seem all that impressed with that particular achievement.

THE BEST INVESTMENT

I've helped thousands of people with their investments, but in the overall scheme of things, is it really important that a group of people is somewhat more prosperous as a result?[1]

Sir John M. Templeton

Over the years, countless Templeton shareholders and brokers have asked John, "What's the best investment?"

He never hesitates to offer this surprising answer: "Tithing."

John has written:

In all my fifty-two years before I retired as an investment counselor, we were helping people, literally hundreds of thousands of people, with their wealth. In all of those years, there was only one investment which never proved faulty, and that was tithing—giving at least 10% of your income to churches and charities. In all my history, I have never seen a family who tithes for as long as ten years that didn't become both prosperous and happy. That is the best investment anyone can select.

And he doesn't mean just money. Twenty-five years ago John made the commitment to donate half of his time to helping people develop their minds and souls. As the mutual funds he managed continued to be honored for their outstanding performance, he essentially proved money management doesn't require a person to be one-dimensional.

A man solely motivated by money would never have established the Templeton Prize for Progress in Religion. John noticed that no Nobel Prizes are given for achievement in that area. So he established his own. It is the world's largest cash prize—for John believes it is the most important subject in the world. Mother Teresa, Billy Graham, Aleksander Solzhenitsyn, Michael Novak, Bill Bright, and Charles Colson have all been among its recipients over the years.

The *Chronicle of Philanthropy* applauded John's

> countless hours of financial advice and fund-raising help to Oxford University (whose business school bears the name of Templeton College), Princeton Theological Seminary, the Presbyterian Church and many other institutions. He is a trustee of some of the world's most revered institutions, including Westminster Abbey.

Templeton was knighted by the Queen Mother in 1987. Those so honored are never told exactly why. But one would assume that John's generous nature was a primary consideration. Now reflect on that for a minute. John Templeton may have made as many superb investments as any person since King Solomon. And he believes the ancients knew exactly what they were doing when they said that if giving time, talent, and money is our very first investment, it will never fail to profit us when done faithfully. John even practices and advocates a double-tithe for those who have reached material and spiritual maturity. In fact, he considers giving to be the mark of the truly mature person. (Interestingly, studies show that economists are twice as likely to give *no* money to churches and charities than the rest of us.) Yet so many people don't seem to have the most basic grasp of the concept that giving equates to maturity. *Why?* Peggy Noonan, President Reagan's favorite speech writer, may have put it poetically. She recently wrote of a special moment of transcendence when she realized that there is more to life than economists can quantify:

I was sure I was being told something, being given a taste of something I could have, if I wanted it. Which I didn't. Or at least I didn't do enough to pursue it. Why wouldn't I take steps that, this moment seemed to suggest, would make this thing, this peace, a part of my life? I don't know. Because it was the unknown, because it would be rigorous, because it would deny me joys I knew, because the compensating joys would be—wholesome. And there is the burden of an ardent nature: I could become good and ruin my life.[2]

To reassure Peggy Noonan and those of us in our darker hours of doubt, here's the bottom line from Templeton: The first step in escaping the burden of an ardent nature that drives us to short-term gains is to give the first 10% of what we are blessed with, including our time and talent. This giving is an indication of true faith that God will provide for our needs and evidence that we are willing to live that faith and have our priorities straight. That makes it the surest initial investment in the development of wealth in all its forms.

ACCUMULATING WEALTH

He who is taught to live upon little owes more to his father's wisdom than he who has a great deal left him does to his father's care.

William Penn

This is another of John's favorite quotes. It deals with an important financial principle that few counselors and clients think about. Namely, if we spend our lives pursuing the goal of accumulated wealth, what will we do with it when it is no longer useful to us? Yet it is critical that we deal with this question. John believes accumulating wealth for its own sake can do more harm than good, and for that reason he practices the double-tithe and plans to give "most" of his accumulated wealth to charities and religious causes. To quote *The Templeton Plan*:

During John Templeton's four decades as an investment counselor, he has seen many families who have left their children great wealth. But that kind of inheritance can create more problems than it solves. In studying hundreds of clients, Templeton has never been able to discern a connection between happiness and inherited wealth. In fact, in most cases the inheritance of wealth has done more harm than good. It tends to give people false values and causes them to show personal pride without having earned that pride. It causes people to take the edge off their efforts.

Personally, I learned the hard way that wealth can even harm the professionals who help people create such wealth. Like many in our profession, I began my career with the sole intent to help people accumulate wealth, which led me to a point of disillusionment and burnout so prevalent in our profession.

At one point, I thought I was helping one of the world's wealthiest men make some important investment decisions. Frankly, he was so wealthy he didn't always know if he was investing his own money, his corporations' money, or the money from one of his banks. So my performance standard was to simply exceed the interest rate he had to pay his bankers. That way, if it was the bank's money, he still made a profit, and if it was his own money, he was also far ahead of the game.

At the end of the first year, I reported that if we had used the bank's money and paid it the prime rate, which was in the mid-teens at the time, my client had still made over $1,000,000—in essence on none of his own money invested. If the money was his own, I had made a return for him that even John Templeton would have been pleased with.

I was proud of that fact. But after I made my report, he simply said, "That's nice," and went back to his work. As I drove home that evening, I asked myself what I had expected. The man already had several hundred million dollars. Did I think I was going to change his life by adding one more? As he had been self-made, did I really think he needed me to tell him how to make money? That was when I realized my professional life was becoming rather meaningless.

In essence, Wall Street practice encourages young brokers to develop business anywhere it can be found but then to discard their smaller accounts as the broker becomes more experienced. That means you usually get rid of the clients who most need the help and, frankly, are usually the most difficult to help.

Yet I now find my greatest joy is in helping widows, retirees, and smaller investors. And when even wealthy people still find me occasionally, I have learned that if we embrace a sense of stewardship and create wealth for the material and spiritual well-being of others, then the process can be far more meaningful and rewarding.

Templeton likes to call any helpful business a "ministry." Naturally, he is particularly fond of the mutual-fund business and views it too as a ministry, and there are good reasons to agree. You may not have thought about it, but the mutual-fund business is one of the most populist and, perhaps, faith-filled enterprises on earth. While many businesses encourage people to spend large amounts of money in instant gratification, the Templeton funds will help anyone with $100 prepare for the future by becoming a part owner of the wealth of our world.

Not only is that important for the individual investor, it provides a foundation crucial to our way of life for all our citizens. Karl Marx believed that the wealthy would eventually own everything in a capitalist economy, but the invention of mutual funds, in my opinion, has helped prove him wrong. As more Americans buy funds, Wall Street and Main Street are increasingly moving in the same direction. I think that is good.

Concern for the average person's economic well-being has been a staple of moral philosophers since the beginning of time. One of the first things Moses did as he led the Israelites toward the Promised Land was to assure that each person would own a little piece of it. In recent years, I have grown to believe that he was right: it *is* very possible that material wealth *can* flow from moral and spiritual principles. But my belief is a little different than that of some of my friends.

As a Christian, I had long appreciated such theologians as C. S. Lewis, who once wrote: "It is since Christians have largely ceased to think of the other world that they have become so ineffective in this. Aim at Heaven and you get earth 'thrown in': aim at earth and you will get neither."[3] Still, I had never met a theologian who had grown materially wealthy on his or her own. So I was a bit skeptical about the idea of "aiming at heaven" and reaping earthly rewards.

Also, my own life experience was no more convincing. Growing up poor, I often felt that the poorer my neighbors were, the more devoutly they nurtured their faith. As I prospered on Wall Street, few of the newly rich I came to know were interested in spiritual matters. It was only when I studied John's life that I truly became a believer.

Now, I am not prepared to say, as many prosperity preachers do, that material wealth *must necessarily flow* or *can only flow* from moral behavior. After studying Uganda and its deeply spiritual people, I regard that philosophy as sheer heresy. I believe that a major reason many Americans no longer appreciate our material blessings is that so many prosperity theologians espouse the illusion that material blessings can flow *only* from moral behavior. When such people correctly perceive that America is in a moral and spiritual depression, they cannot admit to

America's material blessings because that would contradict their flawed theology.

Didn't Christ himself speak of an amazing grace of the economic kind when he said it rains on both the just and the unjust? Didn't pagan Rome thrive for centuries after Christ's disciples failed to attain their mansions on earth? And wouldn't acknowledging the truth that our nation has prospered economically during decades of cultural decline free us to get our priorities straight?

Even so, after studying John's principles, I look to the future and maintain that it is equally heretical to claim that wealth, in all its forms, *cannot* be built on moral and spiritual foundations.

SEEK FIRST . . .

Ethics and spiritual principles should be the basis of everything we do in life. All that we say, all that we think. Every activity should be based on that, including selection of investments. You wouldn't want to be an owner of a company that is producing harm for the public, and therefore, you wouldn't want to be the owner of a share of a company that's producing harm for the public. We should all give great attention to that, and probably it will be profitable to you, because companies that are harmful ordinarily do not prosper for very long. You will be better off with companies that are truly beneficial. They will go up more in price and grow more rapidly.

Sir John M. Templeton

Not too long ago, an acquaintance of mine who worked for a major ministry called me to say that the ministry had implemented a retirement plan for its associates. She had the choice of two stock funds in the growth component of the plan. She asked me to evaluate what activities her money was financing. I replied honestly that several of the top holdings in both funds financed industries the ministry itself had often spoken against. When I asked if they had ever considered ethical issues when choosing their investment options, she replied, sadly, "No."

Most of my Wall Street associates do not care to make ethics a part of their decision-making process—nor did I during most of the early eighties. I could wax eloquent about "alphas, betas, and standard deviations," but if someone asked me if their money was doing something good for someone, I got tongue-tied. Yet deep down I knew that behind all the mathematical facts, diversions, and illusions, real people's lives were being affected, for better or worse, by my investment decisions.

On those rare occasions when someone asked about ethics, I would argue that ethical concerns would probably reduce the return on investment. "If you limit the universe from which you choose your investments," I would explain, "it's only logical you can't make as much money."

FORGIVE THEM, THEY KNOW NOT . . .

Religious belief remains strong but seems to have a diminishing effect on behavior.

Robert Bork

Billy Graham once spoke of the difference between belief and faith. He said that if a man on a highwire asks the crowd below him if they believe he can walk across, everyone on the ground would say, "I believe." If, after walking across the wire once, he takes the handles of a handcart and asks the crowd if they believe he can push it back across, everyone on the ground would say, "I believe." But if he asks, "Who has the faith to get in the handcart?" there would be silence. Faith requires us to put ourselves *into* our beliefs, and that is increasingly viewed as a high-wire act by many of us.

That story summarizes a majority, though certainly not all, of my experiences in religious communities since my first book was published in the early nineties. Many of us live in a community that professes belief in a leader who taught about "two masters" and a "more abundant" life. Yet I am not sure we truly have faith that these concepts still lead to success any longer.

For example, it grieves me to confess that the worst investment I ever made for myself or my clients was created and managed by a man who served on the board of a Christian college. More recently, in another case, the financial press had a good time describing how a group of Lutheran ministers sued their pension board. It seems the pension fund's managers kept an eye on ethics. Their criteria were roughly similar to ones John employed over his remarkable career. But the ministers seemed more interested in the money than in ethics.

The most popular religious mutual-fund advisory newsletter in the country constantly runs articles challenging the importance of ethics in investing. Its publisher, a constant critic of the ethics of those in the public sector, once wrote:

> I receive more questions asking for suggestions on ethical investments than on any other single topic. . . . Unfortunately, I must tell

them I can be of no help. Why not? Because I know of no investments that are guaranteed to meet their criteria. . . . I want to encourage you to shift your thinking away.

He then maintained it was fine to practice ethics when shopping for groceries but not when shopping for investments. Aside from arguing that ethical perfection is not possible in this world, he felt that the individual investor is just too small to make an ethical impact on our culture. Which is true, in a sense. Just as one drug overdose, rape, or abortion doesn't constitute a cultural crisis, one unethical investor won't change our nation. But as more and more people believe that personal behavior doesn't matter, then our culture has a serious problem. As Daniel Webster once said, "The things that are wrong with our country today are the sum total of all the things that are wrong with us as individuals."

Economic Anxiety and Ethics

Several publications have run stories about the nation's first socially *irresponsible* mutual fund. It invests *only* in companies that produce alcoholic beverages, cigarettes, condoms, adult entertainment, sexy lingerie, casino companies, and so on. It is called the Morgan Funshares.

One story says the fund was originally called Morgan Sinshares until the founder met John. "I told him about my fund," the founder recalled, "but he asked me if I knew what sin was. I said yes, sin is what your mother told you not to do. And he said, 'Oh, no, that's not sin.' Then he told me about the seven deadly sins, and he named them—apathy, pride, gluttony—all those bad things. Just after that, I went home and changed the name of the fund."

The founder, so the story says, was quite wealthy but anxious about the economic future. He recalled, "I really just wanted a fund that would be depression proof. I lived through a depression, and it still scares me to death. The theory is that there are certain things that people will not give up, no matter how poor they are. They'll drink to their last nickel, smoke till they are dead."

How is the fund doing in helping investors prepare for the next depression, should it occur? The story said the fund's "share price was up 14.3%, just trailing the Standard & Poor's 500

Index." Yet the story noted the more responsible Domini Social
Equity had returned 30.83% year-to-date.

Financial rewards aside, I had to wonder how much he
might have gained spiritually if, like John, he had known how
much God loves him—and wants him to love others.

We might prosper in many ways by reflecting on a wonderful recent
book by Gertrude Himmelfarb, wife of Irving Kristol, the patriarch of
neoconservatism, and the mother of conservative thinker Bill Kristol.
It is called *The Demoralization of Society*. In one passage, she describes
an author who observed the Jewish community of Victorian London:

> There is no doubt of the powerful impression made upon her by a
> community where, as she saw it, morality infused every aspect of life,
> including the most material and mundane.... It was not the econom-
> ic success of the Jews to which she attributed their superior moral char-
> acter; it was their character that was responsible for their success. (p. 183)

By contrast, Himmelfarb writes of our own time:

> When we now speak of virtue, we no longer think of the classi-
> cal virtues of wisdom, justice, temperance, and courage, or the Chris-
> tian ones of faith, hope, and charity, or even such Victorian ones as
> work, thrift, cleanliness, and self-reliance. Virtue is now understood
> in its sexual connotations of chastity and marital fidelity. (p. 15)

I find this is particularly true of my friends in conservative Christianity. One prominent stewardship leader recently told me that there
was little reason to talk with Catholic leaders as there was little he
could learn from them. I'd offer John Paul's sentiment that "even the
decision to invest in one place rather than another, in one productive
sector than another, is always a moral and cultural choice" as evidence
a little humility might be beneficial. I generally find that we conservatives are most efficient at fundraising, but of limited concsiousness of
the holistic nature of true stewardship.

The *Wall Street Journal* has also noted as much. At the time my first
book was being published, the *Journal* researched several "Christian
financial planners" and claimed they couldn't find that those planners
actually did anything different from anyone else. I would have written
a letter of disagreement—if I could have. But I had to agree instead with
Robert Fitch, dean of the Pacific School of Religion, who wrote:

It will be an interesting matter for later historians to determine the precise point at which ethics became obsolete in our Western Culture. Whatever may be the answer to that question, we may be sure that the researchers will be entertained as they discover the way in which Protestant theology helped toward the obsolescence of ethics.[4]

About a century ago, Christian apologist G. K. Chesterton entered an essay symposium about what was wrong with his country. His entry simply said, "Dear Gentlemen: I am. Sincerely, G. K. Chesterton." I find relatively little of that kind of humility and self-examination today. As Tony Compolo said in the opening pages, most of us seem preoccupied with finding a "them" to demonize. Perhaps that is why Billy Graham also likes to say that the greatest possibilities for ministry are in our own churches, right here in America.

On a more hopeful note, Puritan theologian Jonathan Edwards wrote these words even before the founding of our country:

> The church's extremity has often been God's opportunity for magnifying his power, mercy and faithfulness, towards her. . . . When his church is in a low state, and oppressed by her enemies, and cries to him, he will swiftly fly to her relief, as birds fly at the cry of their young.

OF PROPHETS AND PROFITS

If you select the true spiritual principles, you will attract people to you, no matter what your profession is, particularly if you're in business. You'll have more customers. Your business will grow more rapidly if you work on spiritual principles. So spiritual endeavors and business endeavors go right together. If you try to operate a business without spiritual principles, it will not last long, and you will not do much good in the world.

Sir John M. Templeton

In monitoring the Templeton funds over the years, I have noticed they generally find ways to prosper without financing what Wall Street literally calls the "sin stocks" of alcohol, tobacco, gambling, and adult entertainment companies.

(Surprisingly, I hear that word "sin" as often on Wall Street as in many liberal churches these days. Many Wall Street counselors seem more attuned to the dangers of fear and greed than many conservative ministries. I've noticed that Wall Street often uses the word "stewardship" to mean enabling the poor, ethics, environmental concern, and other matters that are far more holistic in meaning than what usually springs to mind when we hear the word in church or from ministries. As important as institutional development is, might the church be selling a gem of an idea for a few pieces of silver when it turns stewardship into an annual sermon on pledge-card Sunday or the annual telethon?)

I was once with Mark Holowesko, now manager of the largest Templeton funds, after he had just written to the chairman of a major international company. It had an American subsidiary which in turn had a tiny subsidiary making Charles Manson T-shirts. It is doubtful the chairman knew about the tiny operation or that it even showed up in the bottom line of the company. But I had to respect Holowesko for caring enough to bring it to his attention. Who knows? Perhaps one young American will be spared a bit of cultural distraction because of his concern.

John Templeton may have stressed the integration of spiritual principles and investment management, but he would be the first to tell you that he didn't invent ethics among mutual-fund managers. That distinction probably belongs to his friend Phillip Carret of the Pioneer Mutual Fund, founded in 1928. At the request of some religious investors during the 1930s, Pioneer began avoiding the sin stocks, and all Pioneer funds generally maintain that ethic today.

Had you invested $10,000 in the fund at its founding, you would have endured the great depression of the thirties, several wars, inflation, and mountains of federal debt—and still you would have almost $35 million today. That's about 13% annual returns, an incredible rate over the long-run.

Phillip Carret is now ninety-eight, and like John, officially retired. But he is still a favorite commentator on shows like *Wall Street Week*. Many of us still honor his views on investing. He managed the Pioneer Fund for fifty-five years but turned its day-to-day management over to my friend John Carey several years ago. It now has over $2 billion of assets and is still open to investors.*

I once asked John Carey about ethics and he replied:

---

*Your broker or financial planner can tell you about the Pioneer funds, or you can obtain a prospectus by calling 1-800-225-6292. Pioneer Two is the most popular of the Pioneer funds and is one of the largest equity funds in the country. *Morningstar* believes Pioneer Capital Growth Fund is particularly worth considering. Minimum investment is $50.

It has always seemed to me that the integrity of a company's management is an absolute requirement for long-term business success, and that it is the first thing you want to know about a company before making an investment in it. In the short-term, of course, there are all kinds of "quick turnover" ways to make money, both in business and in the stock market—some of which, however, can turn sour in a hurry. But in the long run, companies that act in a responsible way with respect to their employees and customers, their shareholders and the communities in which their facilities are located stand the best chance of succeeding; and their shares will be accorded a premium in the marketplace in the same way that any goods of high quality will sell at better prices.

That's a tremendous statement in an age when, at least, the public perception is that companies only boost profits by laying off people and moving out of local communities. Despite what many Americans think about the ethics of Wall Street professionals, both Carey and Templeton will tell you that many active fund managers deserve as much respect as we owe Phillip Carret.

For example, another fund that has practiced a similar ethic for decades is the $15 billion Washington Mutual Investors Fund, part of the American Funds group, which is chaired by Jon Lovelace. *Forbes* recently quoted Bill Berger of the Berger Funds concerning Lovelace. He said: "There's a reason Jon's been such a success; because he's so modest. If you don't have humility, the market will teach it to you the hard way." *Forbes* concluded the article about Lovelace by commenting, "Leo Durocher was wrong. Not all nice guys finish last."[5] In short, anyone can make money by hurting others. But a truly successful manager makes it by helping others.

Washington Mutual was founded in 1952 to invest in domestic stocks. Had you invested $10,000 at that time and left it alone, it would be worth over $1,700,000 today. Again, that is about 13% annual returns on average. That performance makes it a pretty regular member of the *Forbes* Honor Roll of mutual funds.* And it has grown to be the third largest equity mutual fund in America. *Morningstar* recently gave it one of its top ratings and said this:

---

*You can obtain a Washington Mutual prospectus by calling 1-800-421-4120. Its companion fund, American Mutual, with a similar ethic, rates well with analysts and is one of the largest balanced funds in the country. Minimum investment is $250.

Washington Mutual Investors Fund makes a case for old-fashioned virtues. Guided by the Prudent Investor Rule governing trust fund investing, this fund eschews so-called sin stocks (the tobacco and alcohol businesses) and invests in pillars of the community. Some sniff that moral restrictions lead to reduced returns. This fund's performance flies in the face of such notions.

In recent years, many mutual funds have applied even more extensive ethical standards. While the older funds generally do not mention their ethics (we believe that is because we assume ethics cost us money), the newer funds usually market them. They are often called "socially responsible" funds, as opposed to the "sin stock" funds. They gained considerable acceptance during the Vietnam War when many investors decided they didn't care to profit from the war or from sin stocks.

As with all investing, you have to be discerning but some have done well while doing good. For example, the Pax World Fund is perhaps the best known of the group. It struggled during the early nineties but recently returned to form and has still averaged over 12% returns during the past fifteen years, which is superb for a fund that invests in both stocks and bonds.*

Other funds go beyond the sin stocks and defense issues. The more popular ones are the Calvert group of funds, which is probably the oldest and largest group of socially responsible funds.†

The Parnassus Fund was established a little over a decade ago and has amply rewarded investors with 14% annual returns. Though they have occasionally had bumpy rides along the way, they have still enjoyed some of the highest returns of any socially responsible investors.‡

A bit newer fund is the Domini Social Equity fund which *Morningstar* says "should dominate the socially conscious fund arena. . . . Since inception, this socially screened version of the S&P 500 has kept ahead of the growth-and-income norm and close to the market."** Domini also offers a money-market fund that invests certificates of deposit from the South Shore Bank.

---

*You can obtain a Pax World Fund prospectus by calling 1-800-767-1729. Minimum investment is $250.

†Calvert has several funds. Call 1-800-368-2748 for a prospectus. Minimum investment is $1,000.

‡Call 1-800-999-3505. Minimum Parnassus Fund investment is $2,000.

**Call 1-800-762-6814. Minimum Domini Social Equity investment is $1,000.

The Mennonites have developed the Praxis Funds. (Praxis is a theological term meaning the intersection of belief and practice.) They avoid the defense and sin stocks yet have developed solid track records.*

The Timothy Fund was organized in recent years for religious conservatives. It has too little track record to comment on yet.[†]

More and more funds with specific ethical criteria are being created each year. As they grow, so does the debate about how ethics affect performance. Naturally, most Wall Street analysts and financial publications who don't care to consider ethics maintain they cause sub-par performance. And naturally, most of the studies done by the socially responsible crowd see things in a different light. As Shakespeare once said, it seems "the devil can cite Scripture for his own purpose." Or as Wall Street more graphically puts it, "Figures lie and liars figure."

After nearly a decade of study, however, I have developed two personal opinions. The first is that John Carey is right when he says ethics aren't terribly important for financial success if you are a trader, but they are crucial if you are a true investor. The second is that John Templeton is right when he says ethics should be a primary consideration regardless of how they affect performance.

JUDGE NOT . . .

Let's remember that what is harmful to people is not generally agreed upon. And so, although we have always been careful on that score of ethics, we do not tell people what those ethics are, because we do not have to set ourselves up as a judge against other people who may be in the type of business that we don't think is wise. So, rather than to say what it is, we just practice our ethics without naming.

Sir John M. Templeton

This is a terribly important concept that John brings up. Unless some of the finest minds in the world are wrong, in the very near future more investors will make a renewed effort to actually practice their beliefs. That will be a wonderful thing. But it is also fraught with danger if it isn't kept in proper perspective.

I generally find most people are "absolutist" about integrating ethics and investing. Like one newsletter publisher, they either want absolute

---

*You can order a Praxis Funds prospectus by calling 1-800-503-0905.

[†]You can order a Timothy Fund prospectus by calling 1-800-846-7526. Minimum investment is $1,000.

perfection (Jesus tells us to sell our possessions and give the money to the poor) or absolutely nothing to do with the subject (Jesus said you can't serve two masters). We need to understand that the world is rarely that black and white. Focusing on either extreme usually means we end up avoiding the issue altogether.

Modern corporations and governments are simply groups of people working together on a day-to-day basis. As human beings, they will never be ethically pure, any more than our churches and ministries are. Like them, we investors in corporate and government securities should help one another grow to new levels of ethical behavior, but do it in the true spirit of love, which John calls "the essential ingredient" of any successful endeavor.

WITH YOU ALWAYS . . .

The story is hope and growth. We don't subscribe to the Malthusian disaster scenario.

J. Mark Mobius

As my research into Uganda deepened, I began to take a closer look at what John was doing in the developing nations. I knew he had become associated with a brilliant man by the name of Mark Mobius, who is often referred to as the "Indiana Jones of Wall Street" because he virtually lives on a plane so he can check out companies in remote areas of the world where securities analysts do not congregate. There are even rumors he occasionally commutes to work by way of camel, ox-cart, and sampan.

Mobius's research reveals that 85% of the world's population lives in developing nations, though they account for only 20% of the world's gross domestic product. Despite firsthand knowledge of these poor regions, Mobius refuses to accept the argument of the Reverend Thomas Malthus, who, more than a century ago, predicted that mankind was doomed because our God-given resources could never feed our growing populations. Mobius thinks Malthus is wrong because he sees the economic output of most of those regions growing twice as quickly as the output of the more developed nations, which have denied Malthus by reducing their number of farms as population growth continues. In defense of Malthus, he never imagined anyone would figure out a way for individual investors in richer nations to assist poorer ones.

Mobius manages the Templeton Emerging Markets Fund, which has traded on the New York Stock Exchange since early 1987, and the *Morningstar* report says he has been averaging about 25% annual returns with surprisingly low risk. But Templeton has more recently introduced the Templeton Developing Markets Trust, also managed by Mobius, and John thinks it may be an even better way to invest in developing nations.

Since Uganda did not have a stock exchange, it was difficult for a fund manager to conveniently finance any development of that country at the time. But more developed nations in that region and other regions like Eastern Europe and Latin America did have stock exchanges. So Sherry and I decided that investing up to 10% of our savings in the developing nations might be a useful endeavor.

Like most of the boomer generation, the majority of our savings was in retirement plans. So we calculated that the worst that could happen to us would be to essentially take a tax deduction if we lost the entire amount. That wouldn't be any worse financially than making a charitable contribution. And whether profitable or unprofitable to us, some poorer people around the globe might enjoy better roads, water supplies, and jobs. So we invested a few thousand dollars in the Developing Markets Trust. To our surprise, it increased in value more than 70% that year. It hasn't always done that well, of course, but we are still adding to the fund and have been very pleased with its performance.

We are also pleased with the good we believe we are doing. Some of my well-intentioned friends occasionally argue that we are profiting at the expense of the poor. We disagree. We have generally been pleased with the ventures Mobius has chosen to finance, and we've never taken anything out of those countries. We just reinvest our dividends and capital gains, and he puts them back to work creating opportunities for other people.

There may come a time later in life when Sherry and I need some of that money. It would be fair for us to use what we need at that time. But, like John, I plan to never fully retire so we may never need it. It would be a wonderful thing to name a church or charity the beneficiary of our retirement plans.

CAST YOUR BREAD . . .

We always felt that we were doing good—not only for our investors,
helping them to make more profits—but also for the nations where we

invested. If we send money to buy shares in corporations in the poverty stricken nations, then those corporations can expand more readily and help people. Furthermore, most of those poor nations need infrastructure, such as more pure water, or more telephones, or more highways, and you can't do that by local savings, so you need to have the foreigners to come in and buy shares in order that your infrastructure can be the foundations of the entrepreneurship among the local people.

                                                              Sir John M. Templeton

As I became more knowledgeable about Uganda and other Third World countries, I realized we Americans no longer understand what true poverty is. Studies do indeed say the poor are still among us in America, but many of them now have microwave ovens. In Uganda, by contrast, when we were entertained by the "Margaret Thatcher of Uganda," she prepared dinner for twenty people over an open charcoal fire in her kitchen.

Although the official poverty level in America is dozens of times higher than the average purchasing power of a Ugandan, I do not feel hopeless about their plight. Many observers project that the developing nations may grow twice as quickly as the United States in coming decades. Frankly, before my visit there, I had never thought much about how my personal investments might play a role in that growing prosperity. I used to keep most of my money safely tucked away in the United States, with a small percentage in the other developed nations like Canada, Great Britain, and Australia, simply as a diversification measure for my own benefit. Most Americans do the same. A few years ago, John told Louis Rukeyser, "The American public has only about 6% of its total assets outside America, whereas 65% of all the stocks in the world are outside of America." We invest even less today. Even a tiny change there could make a world of difference.

THE LEAST OF THESE . . .

There will always be opportunities to give to less fortunate people. Now, there's no easy way to help them but one of the best ways is to help them to learn how to operate some business of their own, or some other activity of their own. Then they become self-supporting, and thereby they learn not to be just getters from other people, but to be givers of their talents to others.

                                                              Sir John M. Templeton

We might even bequeath those funds to an organization that would keep them creating wealth in the Third World after we are gone.

Several years ago, a friend asked if I would truly like to help the very poorest people on earth. I guess I looked skeptical, for he added he wasn't talking about giving the proverbial fish, which can inadvertently lead to good feelings for the donor but dependency for the recipient. He explained that he was talking about giving the fishing pole instead, along with instructions on how to catch fish, in order to enable the poor to become self-sufficient. This intrigued me.

While we were in Uganda, one of my new friends said in a moment of rare candor, "Every year, you Americans come here and ask what you can do to help us. Every year, we reply, 'Give us jobs.' And every year you go back, and your government sends bureaucrats, and your churches send missionaries. That's good for the employment of Americans, but it doesn't do much for us." I had heard that story before. So I listened as my friend told me about a Christian-based organization in Chicago called Opportunity International. It is a global network that makes business loans as small as $50 to the poorest of the poor in the Third World nations—many of which are only dreaming of having a stock exchange one day.

The process starts with successful business people making donations to the network. Those donations are then often matched by governments and other institutional donors. The money is then transferred to agencies headed by other volunteer business people within the various Third World nations. They make the decisions about who has a viable project that justifies a loan; they provide basic training in accounting and other business skills; they teach the basic moral responsibilities of managing wealth; and then they make and monitor the loan.

As we discovered in Uganda, most of the world's desperately poor are women, so it might be a $50 loan to a widow to buy a used sewing machine or an oven for baking. This allows her to work at home, watch her children, and still put food on the table. Or it might be a loan so a poor person can start a small manufacturing business. Both may eventually employ one, two, or more neighbors, as the projects are limited only by the creativity of the person involved.

The financing vehicle is a loan, so that when the businesses become successful, the loans are to be repaid so the process can start all over again with other poor people. The repayment rate averages about 95%, considerably higher than the rate of American students who repay college loans. It is no exaggeration to say that a small loan is an investment that can change the lives of many people in the Third World. It has even happened here in the states.

Bob Galvin, chairman of the executive committee of Motorola, is a friend of, and donor to, Opportunity International. His father started Motorola with $500, the size of the average Opportunity loan. Like most of the borrowers at Opportunity, Galvin's first loans were not secured by assets. They were secured by the character of the borrower. Tens of thousands of current Motorola shareholders, employees, and customers can be grateful someone had the faith to make such loans. Bob Galvin is helping to pass that chance on to others. He has said, "Opportunity International reinforces our faith in human nature throughout the world. People everywhere thrive on opportunity. Opportunity International provides that welcome chance."

In recent years, these ventures have increasingly been called "micro-enterprise." While short of perfection, they are changing the way foreign aid has been practiced in the past. And that brings up an important point we have to deal with daily in our ministries.

Surveys tell us a large percentage of Americans think foreign aid is a major item in the U.S. budget. That is simply another most unfortunate illusion of political rhetoric. In reality, the U.S. gives a lower percentage of its national income to foreign aid than any major nation on earth. In discussing efforts to eliminate much or all of that foreign aid, the *Economist* said, "Aid is not popular (opinion polls show that most people think at least 15% of the federal budget is spent on foreign aid; in fact the $16 billion spent is only 1% of the budget and less than 0.3% of GDP)."[6]

Nevertheless, one of the promising trends is that our government has reduced the amount of money it sends directly to foreign governments and has begun utilizing organizations like Opportunity to channel money more directly to the poor. A *Reader's Digest* article has said, "By funding enterprising individuals rather than monolithic states, Opportunity's remarkable partnership is revolutionizing the fight against poverty around the world."

John, already a donor, recently agreed to become a spokesperson for Opportunity. During a taping session he said,

> I'm really thrilled and excited by Opportunity International, that's helping people to become entrepreneurs. In that way, they not

only help them economically, but they help them spiritually. They help them to have more self-respect, more feelings of independence, more self-esteem and also to be of benefit to the nation, because a nation prospers depending on how many people have those virtues.

Among those on the board of advisers are Millard Fuller of Habitat for Humanity, Bob Seiple of World Vision, and religious historian Martin Marty. I am privileged to serve on its board as well. It has been one of the most enlightening and rewarding activities I have ever engaged in.*

THE MANY REWARDS

The developed countries also have a tremendous stake in the Third World. Unless there is rapid development there—both economic and social—the developed countries will be inundated by a human flood of Third World immigrants far beyond their economic, social or cultural capacity to absorb.

Peter Drucker, *Post-Capitalist Society*

Many people cannot grasp why I invest my time and money in helping to develop the Third World. As always, my motivation is spiritual and financial. I have come to believe they cannot be compartmentalized.

The spiritual motivation comes from my Christian belief, which means my success is not defined by making someone's list of the wealthiest people on earth. It is defined by Christ. And he said he would judge my success by how many of "the least of these" I have fed, given water to, and clothed. While America has its own "poor," the majority of "the least of these" are actually in the Third World.

But my motivation is also financial. It is difficult for us to imagine the immensity of the challenges in the Third World, but it is also difficult to imagine the opportunities for those who are willing to meet those challenges.

Describing why he invested heavily in domestic and international oil companies last year, Mark Holowesko recently said:

In the U.S., people drive their cars a lot and consume over 23 barrels of oil per person per year. India and China consume less than one barrel of oil per person per year. Meanwhile, just across the Formosa Straits in Taiwan, they consume 11 barrels per person per year. Sup-

---

*Opportunity International invites inquiries about joining our efforts. Call 1-800-793-9455.

pose that India and China got to ony 1/2 the level of Taiwan. The incremental demand from those two counties alone would be equivalent to the current output of OPEC.

Money manager Jim Rogers recently wrote,

A current goal of the Chinese government is that each resident receive one more egg every four days. The extra chickens required to achieve this goal will annually consume the equivalent of the entire grain crop of Australia, itself one of the world's largest grain-producing countries.[7]

Meanwhile, a recent *Forbes* article observed:

Between 1992 and 1994, personal computer sales in the U.S. rose 44%, to $37 billion. The Western European market, meanwhile, grew only 22%. Now look at the emerging markets. Personal computer sales there grew 83% between 1992 and 1994. At $22 billion, emerging markets now account for nearly a quarter of global PC sales.[8]

Over the years, I have experimented with several investment philosophies. In the early years, I practiced a fairly pure form of investment. I looked at investments purely for my own benefit. And I scanned the yields and performance charts for pure performance.

But during the crash of 1987, I learned the hard way that performance can be enhanced through prudence, which includes both conservative investments and patience.

In more recent years, I have even learned that risk can be further reduced by elevating ethics and financing the true needs of my neighbors around the world. I now call ethics, prudence, and performance my ABCs of investing. They are complementary, rather than in conflict.

Of course, this more mature approach can be largely credited to John Templeton. He often says that if we take our focus off ourselves and help others in the best way we can, the rewards will eventually follow. I don't know what the future holds, but I do know that practicing this golden rule of investing has enriched my life both spiritually and financially. After twenty years of investment counseling, it is the only financial advice I can offer without any reservation whatsoever.

nine

MONEY, MORALITY, AND A NEW MILLENNIUM

GOLDEN RULE:
Looking Out for Number One,
Doesn't Make You Number One

So we fix our eyes not on what is seen, but on what is unseen. For what is seen is temporary, but what is unseen is eternal.

(2 Corinthians 4:18)

John Calvin taught that people will instinctively worship, but if not taught to worship God, they will create idols to worship. Today more people worship idols than God, and those idols are often the institutions and governments created by men themselves.

Sir John M. Templeton

*J*ohn Templeton once told me that the greatest spiritual challenge of his life was learning to love Joseph Stalin. I must have looked surprised, but I gradually understood. John believes that life is a school for the spirit, instructing us and testing us to see if we can handle its challenges without anger or losing our faith, hope, and charity. While John hates the things Stalin did to tens of millions of people, he also tries to live the teaching of Jesus by loving his neighbor—even his enemy. It is an old challenge of the Christian life to hate the sin but love the sinner, and John sincerely believes Jesus challenges us to do that—without exception.

Shortly after that conversation with John, I attended a business function at which someone asked me if I thought John was "really a Christian." I replied as I would have if I had been asked about Billy Graham, Pope John Paul, Mother Teresa, or Pat Robertson: "God alone knows." But the serious expression of the inquirer prompted me to ask his reasons for wondering. He said that though Templeton has devoted virtually all his time and talent, as well as most of his money, to progress in religion, he rarely talks about his Christian belief. Others have expressed the same concern. (I wish they could see John's interview on the Canadian television show called CrossCurrents. In a scene that would probably be edited in the U.S., he spoke about Christ and the Bible being the greatest influences of his life.) Furthermore, neither liberals nor conservatives are able to pigeon-hole him into one camp or the other. And others don't think he is "American" enough.

So I began to reflect on the fact that many Christians today talk about Jesus but don't model his behavior. (Christians are often accused of preferring faith to works; more often I think we prefer words to works. We might reflect on John 14:12.) Though Jesus said we would be able to recognize his disciples by their love for one another, many of us find it difficult to love Christians in other denominations, of other lands, or of different political persuasions—much less atheists and communists. But to understand John's belief that true success is a loving state of mind, we need to take a hard look at the thinking that shapes both the virtues and the failings of people—many of whom are dedicated Christians—on both the liberal and conservative ends of the political and theological spectrum. I pray that you read this not as yet another cause for division but as a plea for frail and diverse humans beings to come together as the Master intended.

WORSHIPING GOVERNMENTS AND MARKETS

There are those who say that conservatives must make a choice between a message of economic growth and a message of cultural renewal. Take your side, we are told, and the fight can begin. Make your decision between economics and cultural values. Moments like this call for clarity. So I want to argue as directly as I can: This choice is false. It is false in the realm of ideas because it ignores the full range of human needs.

Jack Kemp, *Imprimis* (August 1994)

Rush Limbaugh once published a political cartoon of a man bowing down to a statue of Karl Marx. The man was labeled "The Religious Left." I thought the cartoon arrogant and divisive—even by Limbaugh's standards. (Perhaps that is why a recent survey said, "Many Bible believing Christians see political liberals as the enemy. Two-thirds of the most conservative believers say it is difficult to be both a political liberal and a true Christian" [*Christianity Today*, April 29, 1996.]) Still, I have to agree that many of my liberal friends would do well to reflect on a remark by Sir John Templeton: "Never did Jesus advocate government welfare for the poor!" He went on to say:

> A century ago governments in general, particularly America's, had no responsibility for the poor. But now they do, which is a wonderful thing. Consequently, there is not the great need that there once was. But it would have been better spiritually if that had not happened. It would have been better spiritually if the people had been giving individually through their churches or other charity organizations, or person to person. Because by doing it through government, you lose the joy of giving. Maybe the recipient will be just as well off, but the giver is better off if he does the giving instead of having the government do it for him.

In other words, at times the religious left may be at risk of gaining the world but losing its soul by mixing the thoughts of Jesus and Marx. I could write more about this trend among liberal thinkers, but I suspect the idea is already familiar to most of my readers. What may not be as obvious is that conservative thinkers make a similar mistake— one that may be every bit as damaging.

Conservatives too are guilty of confusing secular philosophies with religion—a practice theologians call "syncretism," and in the vanguard of conservative syncretism are those who often inadvertently embrace the thought of Ayn Rand, a woman of profound influence on America's political economy. Though many people have never even heard of her, she was the only woman listed in the *Economist's* recent "Good Guru Guide,"[1] which said:

> Ayn Rand—the heroine of America's libertarian right—argued that big business was "America's persecuted minority." Rand died in 1982. Her philosophy thrives and her books still sell half a million copies a year, thanks to a plethora of outfits designed to acquaint the world with her thoughts. Rand labeled her philosophy objectivism and

described it as "the concept of man as a heroic being, with his own happiness as the moral purpose of his life, with productive achievement as his noblest activity, and reason as his only absolute."

The Reagan presidency provided opportunities for a few objectivists to try their hand at their most hated institution: government. The most celebrated Randist even survived the passing of the Reagan years. Alan Greenspan, chairman of the Federal Reserve, was an acolyte of Rand's in the 1960s. Presumably he no longer believes Rand's argument that "every government interference in the economy consists of giving an unearned benefit, extorted by force, to some men at the expense of others."

If we are ever to reduce the role of government without causing anarchy in our financial future, we need to subject Rand's version of conservative thought to some serious examination, for I believe it may explain some rather ungodly thinking that may be shaping the America our children will inherit. Such examination may also explain why many leading Republicans, who say they are "fiscal conservatives with a social conscience," aren't totally sure that either political party can stake a claim to absolute truth. As my fellow conservatives read along, ask yourself the question: As others look at my life, rather than listen to my beliefs, would they see the influence of Jesus or Ayn Rand? (I trust my liberal friends will read with empathy and ask, "Jesus or Marx" about their own lives.)

Every few weeks an ad in the *Economist* refers to Rand as a "prophetic genius" whose concepts have "sparked a fire in the hearts, minds and hands of a new generation of prime movers." It invites readers to inquire about seven utopian communities around the world that offer life "without government rule," which would be fine, I guess, except that many of her disciples are prime movers not only in the government itself but in our national thinking about our life together here in the United States. The idea that utopia can be achieved by simply eliminating government demands serious reflection.

FOCUSING ON THE ETERNAL UNSEEN...

Education which stops with efficiency may prove the greatest menace to society. The most dangerous criminal may be the man gifted with reason, but with no morals.

The Rev. Dr. Martin Luther King Jr.

At one point in the Bible (1 Samuel 8), when the people of Israel come to the aged prophet Samuel to demand that he give them an earthly king, Samuel warns them of the tremendous economic burden that will mean. Certainly, big government has always been a burden on our economic well-being. But we forget to consider this: minimal government oversight of morally confused people can be a burden on our economic resources as well. Take the savings-and-loan bailouts, the limited partnership failures, the junk bonds defaults, and the collapsed insurance companies that we experienced during the eighties. Randist, anti-government thought played a major role in creating those disasters and their resulting financial burdens. And yet, in spite of its failures, such thinking may actually be gaining more influence than ever.

Federal Reserve Board Chairman Alan Greenspan was featured in the cover story of *Worth* magazine called "Playing God at the Fed." It is definitely worth a trip to the library, as a more recent issue of *Worth* warns: "We seem to be moving from a world of seller beware to one of buyer beware" in the regulation of the investment world again. The first story began, "Alan Greenspan seems to believe we should all just butt out and let him run the world's economy. His mentor, Ayn Rand, would approve, but others would find it more troubling."[2] It goes on to describe how Rand, who was in the front row at the White House when Greenspan was sworn in, "must have been amused by the sight of the ardent atheist placing his right hand on a Talmud." The story noted that Greenspan later denied the great "I Am" of Judeo-Christian reality by saying, "I think I exist but I can't be certain. In fact I can't be certain that anything exists." I don't know about you, but I would feel better knowing that the man who most influences my financial future knows that I exist.

The story goes on to detail Greenspan's "love of free markets, deep suspicion of do-gooders and righteous hatred of the state apparatus." It says he "masterminded a proposal to set Wall Street free from regulation" as the stock market went into frenzy in 1968 and crashed in the next few years. It then details how he almost single-handedly deregulated the savings-and-loan industry during the eighties while serving as a consultant for Charles Keating of Lincoln Savings and Loan infamy. The article concludes, "What he couldn't imagine was that freeing heroes such as Charles Keating from the shackles of bureaucracy would only make matters worse. It was a prime example of how the Randian view can collide with reality."

French philosopher Blaise Pascal once said reality is that man is created neither beast nor angel. If everyone in the free marketplace were angels, as Rand and Greenspan seemed to believe, we could free the Keatings of the world and they would behave themselves. But such an expectation is unreal. After all, one of Rand's own books was titled *The Virtue of Selfishness*.

Hollywood conservative Arnold Schwartzenegger personally endorses Rand's books and testifies that her thinking changed his life. You may remember that Schwartzenegger stood beside George Bush as he accepted the Republican Party's nomination at the rather low-spirited Houston convention in 1992. I have often pondered whether his presence on the platform didn't signal that the "kinder, gentler" approach of George Bush was being replaced by the more "survival of the fittest" mentality of the Randists. Many observers have suggested that the harsher spirit of Bush's second presidential campaign may have helped to boost Bill Clinton into the White House.

Convicted junk-bond king Michael Milken is another disciple of Rand. *Barrons* interviewed him while he was serving time in prison and commented:

> The interview is valuable in one sense, in that it warns the rest of us about what Milken has been spending his time in prison doing: re-reading Ayn Rand. If Milken still commands a personal fortune of more than $1 billion, and if Milken has been spending his time in the slammer re-reading Ayn Rand, we all have serious cause to worry some months hence, when Milken is sprung.[3]

Of course, Milken has been sprung. Recently he has been helping to shape mega-media companies like Time-Warner—companies that will, in turn, shape your children's thinking well into the next millennium.

A number of revolutionaries in the U.S. House of Representatives have also been influenced by Rand's thinking. They often rally behind Majority Leader Dick Armey, who even has a doctorate in economics. As the *Wall Street Journal* has noted, "Libertarians tend to think that the best way to accomplish good things, economic or social, is simply to get government out of the way. . . . Rep. Armey tends toward libertarian thinking."[4]

Armey likes to invent what have come to be called Armey's Axioms. For example, "Markets are rational, government is dumb." Thinking like that certainly suggests he has been reading too many books influenced by Ayn Rand and too few by the Founding Fathers, who often made great sacrifices in their personal lives to establish our government in the first place. Armey's axiom reminds us that putting libertarians in charge of Congress is a little like putting atheists in charge of a seminary. Not only will it stop the growth of the institution but it may also inhibit its primary function—which is to regulate those who lack the social conscience to consider your well-being as they pursue their own.

Armey and his fellow revolutionaries have also been influenced by the libertarian Cato Institute, which the *Wall Street Journal* calls "a think tank considered to have much influence over the rebellious mood of the new Republican Congress." The Cato Institute, it added, is headed by "Ed Crane, the canny, plumpish fifty-year-old former Libertarian Party boss."

MODERATION IN ALL THINGS

Though many voters probably don't even realize it, much of the angry sentiment coursing through their veins today isn't traditionally Republican or even conservative. It's libertarian . . . utterly disdainful of government.
                                    The Wall Street Journal (January 20, 1995)

To understand the world's political economies, imagine a line running from left to right.

Communists would be on the radical left end of the line. These people were an intellectual elite who thought they could engineer a utopia on earth as long as the government managed everything in the political economy. Notice I used the past tense. Communism seems comatose and may have finally died beneath the ruins of the Berlin Wall, which was built on its shaky moral foundations.

In the middle of the line is what we call socialist thought. It is prevalent in the nations where governments control about half of the economy through taxation and spending. Many nations are rethinking this model as well.

About two-thirds of the way to the right are the "mixed economies" or capitalist democracies—like the United States, Japan, and Australia—in which private citizens still make most of the economic decisions. In the past, believers in this system of economy have been called "conservatives." Curiously, however, those who believe in this form of economy and work to maintain the present balance between private and government control are increasingly called "liberals" in today's political environment. The *Wall Street Journal* recently said many of these liberals are Republican members of Congress who have always thought of themselves as traditionalists. Moderates too seem to be passing into the history books as they rethink government welfare, social security, and other issues.

A little farther to the right are the neoconservatives—that is, the "new" conservatives. These are people who would like to see the government less involved in the economy, especially in the area of middle-class and corporate entitlements. While they respect the intentions of federal planners, they also worry about unintended consequences of too much control. The road to hell, they would suggest, is paved with good over-regulated intentions.

While liberals might quote the biblical story of Joseph—who stored a portion of the people's grain during seven fat years and accepted their gratitude during the seven lean ones—neoconservatives remember the rest of the story—that this plan led to bondage for coming generations. That is a lesson that we too are now learning as we deal with our welfare, Social Security, and Medicare problems. While neoconservatives may sometimes consider big government to be a product of human folly, they do not usually believe, as the Randists do, that it is the root of all evil. Neoconservatives may believe the free market can satisfy people's material needs, but they don't expect it to create heaven on earth by meeting all human needs.

Neoconservatives generally believe that religion is essential to a culture. They believe religion can help regulate market behavior through the internal mechanism of personal virtue; though when that internal regulation fails, they accept the need for government to regulate behavior through external coercion. That is not a very pretty picture, of course, but it beats anarchy.

That brings us to the radical right-hand end of the line: the libertarians. (Actually, there are some libertarians on the left who want government to cease functions like the military, but they are hardly the political force today that they were in the sixties.) Libertarians usually have an absolute faith in the free market. They are theologically certain that government is the giant that prevents us from entering the promised land, so they sling a lot of stones to cut it down to size and wouldn't mind beheading it. Aside from manipulating political alliances with religious conservatives for their own purposes, they have about as much use for traditional religion as Karl Marx did. In their view, the Judeo-Christian teaching of "moderation in all things" is entirely too tolerant of government. (They would hardly appreciate Romans

13.) And religion's moral constraints can conflict with their belief in the absolute freedom of the individual.

Conservatives often attribute the rampant individualism and social turbulence of the sixties to the liberals. But it is interesting to note that at that time Ayn Rand was hardly a paragon of traditional values. She had a public and messy affair with Nathaniel Branden, her closest disciple, who was young enough to be her son. Being rational people who determined their own sense of right and wrong, they simply asked Rand's husband and Branden's wife to leave the house one day a week. This went on for over a decade. But then Branden had an affair with another woman, famously described as "someone not old enough to be his mother." Ironically, Rand excommunicated him from their group.

Also, there has been considerable speculation that Rand used drugs—which wouldn't be too surprising since leading libertarians have long advocated the legalization of street drugs.

In the words of one political analyst,

> Libertarianism is a philosophy of radically limited government. . . . It is attractive to those well-off professionals who have nothing in common with the religious right but would just like to be left alone. . . . The libertarians have also replaced the Marxists as the world's leading utopia builders.[5]

Obviously, I sound harsh toward libertarians. But my point is not to be judgmental as much as to make religious conservatives aware that the secularism they seek to combat does not emanate entirely from the left side of the political spectrum. Just because we disagree with those on the left does not mean that everyone on the right shares our values. By the same token, this understanding may even encourage us to stop pointing our fingers at the religious left and start extending our hands to them. Many of them may be our best allies in meeting the secularist and humanist challenges in our future.

TO THE LEFT, TO THE RIGHT, OR STRAIGHT ABOVE?

Be very strong; be careful to obey all that is written in the Book of the Law of Moses, without turning aside to the right or to the left.

Joshua 23:6

Many politically conservative religious leaders take it as an article of faith that Rand's philosophy will help usher in the kingdom of God.

Yet they seem to forget many of the political lessons of the Bible. Moses was a lawmaker, plain and simple; King David was a political leader of great honor; Jesus refused to join the zealots in their effort to overthrow the unjust government of their day; and both Peter and Paul said Christians should honor the pagan political authority of Rome.

In short, the Bible nowhere endorses the creation of an earthly utopia by the throwing off of governmental rule. Yet many people I counsel do endorse such a concept, and I believe their expectations of such a utopia are frustrating their journey to success. It is just one of those unrealistic expectations that will leave us disappointed when we discover it is out of touch with reality. Yet, it seems even many Christians are forgetting that this world is not our home but simply a training ground for better things to come.

Take Pat Robertson, for example. He has written, "The aim of free people everywhere is to limit the power and the scope of the government in any way they can."[6] I can't imagine a more explicitly anti-government, libertarian thought, and I also think that phrase "any way they can" is potentially quite dangerous.

Ralph Reed, the executive director of the Christian Coalition, echoes the same thoughts, though he moderates his rhetoric somewhat. In the *Wall Street Journal* he wrote, "Traditionalist ends can be advanced through libertarian means."[7] In essence, he seems to be saying that it is justifiable to stir up feelings of hatred toward the government in order to move the country a little more to the right. Again, that approach seems careless at best and, at its worst, irresponsible, atheistic, and anti-Christian.

Then there is Pat Buchanan, another pessimistic media-personality-turned-politician who would like to save us. He is a curious synthesis of anti-government sentiment and a desire for politicians to determine how we invest, who we trade with, and who we hire. In a recent editorial entitled "An American Economy for Americans," Buchanan lamented the desperate condition of the American economy and suggested that we should "work, save and invest here in the land of the free. . . . Let's replace ties with foreigners with ties among Americans."[8] While Buchanan might agree with the old Sunday school song that "Jesus Loves the Little Children of the World," he obviously does not intend for us to love them as Jesus did—at least in financial ways. That may be good politics, but it is bad economics. (God will judge its morality.)

Just a few days after Buchanan's comments were published, Robert Lucas accepted the Nobel Prize for Economics. He has an entirely different perspective on our economy: "The U.S. is a low-inflation country without major unemployment. We're doing great, and have been for a long time."[9] Buchanan seems to be unaware that the United States receives more than twice as much "foreign direct investment" from other nations—more than ten times as much as Japan—than any other country. That is one reason our exports are growing far faster than any other major nation.

All this suggests that Buchanan's politically motivated philosophy might even be harmful to your soul. On a more temporal level, it could also be dangerous to our economy and your personal financial success in the not-too-distant future. The U.S. stock market may soon reach the stage of greedy euphoria that typically accompanies market peaks. (The Templeton funds moved from their heavily overweighted position in the U.S. to one that is underweighted as our stock market streaked toward the 6000 level in early 1996.) That euphoria will probably occur when most of us finally see through the political smoke and realize the American economy is in fact number one and has been—"for a long time."

At that point, adopting Buchanan's isolationist thinking might lead to your losing money in overpriced U.S. stocks rather than making money in underpriced stocks around the world. More success will probably come from Templeton's philosophy of loving the little children of the world rather than flirting with the Randian philosophy of looking out for number one.

I am not convinced that economic nationalism is good for our nation. While Buchanan once described himself as the greatest free-trade advocate in the Reagan White House, the *Economist* has noted that his thinking changed with the political polls during the difficult economic transition of the early nineties:

> Before the second world war, it was Republicans who stood for protection and Democrats for free trade. Indeed, it is often forgotten that Reed Smoot and Willis Hawley, champions of the punitive tariff, were members of the Grand Old Party; and that it was Roosevelt's secretary of state, Cordell Hull, who was mostly responsible for undoing the damage they did. (Note: Many economists believe their desire to build an economic wall around America played a major role in bringing on the Great Depression.) Those protectionist leanings never disappeared among Republicans, recently cropping up most

visibly on the nationalist, far right wing of the party in the persons of Mr. Buchanan and Jesse Helms.[10]

HUMAN LIMITATIONS

Ordinary mortals often judge the value of economists on their ability to forecast accurately the next recession. Governments, in turn, are judged by voters on their ability to avoid it. And on both tests, economists and governments seem repeatedly to have failed. In fact, the ability to forecast (or, still better, to prevent) recessions is a bad test of the worth of anybody.

The Economist

That doesn't seem like the America I grew up in. In the fifties, my father seemed to have a different job or start a different business every few years, and he thought it perfectly normal. The media and politicians had not told him he was in the "anxious class," so he just confidently worked us into the middle class. Everyone I knew thought he was a success. Yet today we seem to expect somebody to do something that will give us perpetual security, which may be why Wall Street entices us with "securities" and the government promises us "Social Security." But even the ancients knew there is no security in secular and human affairs. That is a divine proposition.

So I wonder why so many Republicans are attracted to what is often called "root-canal economics," which says that if we want the minor pain of layoffs and sluggish growth to stop hurting us, we have to perform major, painful surgery on the economy. Frankly, I have never understood that prescription. I am sure there are times when our economy can use a checkup. But as long as respected, conservative economists say we are the richest, freest nation on earth, I can see little reason for attempting major surgery, especially when politicians prescribe that they would like to attempt it—without anesthetic. These politically inspired sentiments may be why Billy Graham once remarked, "I'm conservative theologically, but I don't consider myself on the religious right."[11]

Traditional conservatives, by contrast, know that overthrowing the government, building a wall around America, and looking out for number one won't create a utopia. Unlike Ralph Reed, we believe that traditionalist ends are best advanced through traditionalist means— like more religion of the biblical variety, more focused on love, virtue, and charity than on political activity. As a result, we are less angry, more at peace with our neighbors, and more hopeful about the future of our country and world. And we believe this spiritual peace is more likely to lead to material blessings.

As our country approaches the Third Millennium in a more conservative mood, it might be timely to spend a few minutes comparing, point by point, Ayn Rand's objectivism with John Templeton's traditionalism, for these forces could determine what kind of America our children will inherit.

IDEAS ABOUT GOD, MAN, AND THE WORLD

Over the years, I've been convinced nothing exists except God. There is no other reality.

Sir John M. Templeton

Faith is a malignancy that no system can tolerate.

Nathaniel Branden

A primary tenet of Rand's and Branden's philosophy is that reason is the "only absolute." This is Enlightenment rationalism at its purest. While Rand taught that everyone should live according to their own conscience, the truth is that she could not tolerate anyone in her commune who differed from her views. Like Marx, Rand was a devoted atheist who essentially created her own secular religion to suit her purely materialistic version of reality. She referred to traditional religious people as "mystics and sacrificial animals"—people who could feel but not think. While Jesus asks us to love God with all our heart, soul, and *mind*, Rand asserted that this inability to think explains the religious person's dependence on the revelations of Scripture and on the great minds of the past.

John Templeton's basic philosophy, on the other hand, speaks of "the inadequacy of our senses and intellect to fully comprehend.... Intelligence, logic, is a gift from God, but it's very limited." In other words, while John may value the human mind, he thinks it is irrational to make of it a god.

Once Rand convinced herself that traditional religion is wrong about the existence of God, she had to create her own concepts of what it means to be human. While traditional religion says that we are created in the image of God, Rand insisted that man's goal is to reshape "the earth in the image of his values."

The Scriptures teach that Jesus was the ideal human, but Rand's bible, her novel called *Atlas Shrugged*, says her ideal human was named John Galt. We will get back to him later.

IDEAS ABOUT OUR NEIGHBOR

I think that God supplies all of our needs if we are trying to help other people, so we do not need to be too concerned about our own welfare.
Sir John M. Templeton

The idea that man's self-interest can be served only by a non-sacrificial relationship with others has never occurred to those humanitarian apostles of unselfishness, who proclaim their desire to achieve the brotherhood of men.
Ayn Rand

Like Marx, Rand's thinking cut the heart out of mankind. While Saint Augustine may once have said that the heart contains a God-shaped vacuum that can only be filled with God, Ayn Rand thought that if God had ever existed, he was now dead, so there was no longer any need to love our neighbors as ourselves. Instead, we were to self-ishly love "our own happiness as the moral purpose of our lives."

In her book *The Virtue of Selfishness*, Rand explained the role of humanitarianism in her philosophy:

> It is only in emergency situations that one should volunteer to help strangers, if it's in one's power. For instance, a man who values human life and is caught in a shipwreck, should help to save his fellow passengers—though not at the expense of his own life. But this does not mean that after they all reach shore, he should devote his efforts to saving his fellow passengers from poverty, ignorance, neurosis or whatever other troubles they might have.[12]

If taken seriously by public officials, such a philosophy would have enormous public policy implications. The problem is that some do take it very seriously. For example, do you remember the entertainers Sonny and Cher? Sonny, as you may know, is now a congressman. The *Wall Street Journal* has said this about his concern for others, "I've got mine, Babe: GOP Rep. Sonny Bono, lamenting bashing of the rich, says, 'Nobody handed me anything. I don't think I have to share it with anyone. I did it, and it's mine.'"[13]

Combine Rand's metaphor of the shipwreck with Congressman Bono's thoughts about sharing with the poor and you'll understand why the normally conservative columnist George Will wrote that current efforts at budget balancing have given "a whole new meaning to the phrase: women and children first."[14]

Yet Randist thinking also afflicts the more fortunate. *Worth* said this about Chairman Greenspan:

> Referring to the disastrous advice given by a Merrill Lynch broker who sucked nearly $100 million in commissions from Orange County, Greenspan declares that both brokers and their customers should be "unburdened by any perceived need to take into consideration the interest of their counterparties." It sounds dull enough— until you realize what he's driving at. Greenspan expressed that same radical belief more clearly during the 1960s in a book of essays assembled by his mentor, the novelist and free-market zealot, Ayn Rand.

Are you still with me? The most powerful economic player in the world today does not believe that your financial advisers need to consider your interests—and he doesn't believe you need to consider their interests either. Nor do you and your adviser, by extension, need to consider the interests of your neighbors or future generations. It is every man for himself.

Greenspan spoke those words before Congress, and yet there is no evidence that anyone in Congress challenged the chairman's philosophy. Some may have actually nodded in agreement since another of Congressman Armey's axioms is: "Social responsibility is a euphemism for personal irresponsibility." In other words, if Good Samaritans would just stop caring for others along the road of life, they would have to take care of themselves.

Do you see why I believe this thinking may influence the America your children will inherit? Consider this interview by columnist David Broder:

> I asked Armey if he believed sufficiently in the morality of the marketplace to dissent from the many Republicans and conservatives who have been calling on the TV, movie and record industries to stop producing material celebrating violence and degrading women. He said that he personally didn't care for much of the popular fare on the market today and wondered why there couldn't be more Lion Kings. But as a man of influence, he would not jawbone those executives. Why? Because, he said, "If I run a movie company, my job is to sell movies." And then he leaned across a plate of fajitas and quoted an axiom he attributed to Andrew Carnegie but which

actually was uttered by another nineteenth century tycoon, railroad magnate William H. Vanderbilt: "The public be damned! I work for my stockholders." If that isn't a slogan for our time, then Dick Armey and his disciples would not be writing the nation's laws.[15]

Ironically, many religious conservatives who put Armey in power are now wondering if corporate leaders shouldn't consider employees and communities as well as shareholders.

This attitude is also associated with Milton Friedman and the Chicago School of Economics. Friedman was probably the most influential economist of the eighties and Senator Phil Gramm recently named him the economic policy adviser he would most listen to if elected president. Friedman is often quoted for his statement that "our only social responsibility is to make money. Period." In other words, if the Good Samaritan had simply gone back to work and made money, everything would have been just fine.

David Selbourne, a best-selling social critic in Britain, has written: "Milton Friedman has done more damage to the concept of civic good than any previous political or economic philosopher. . . . You cannot remoralize citizen behavior when the civic order itself is being sold."[16]

Fortunately, economist Peter Drucker, who is respected by many of us in traditional religious circles, has written: "It is futile to argue, as does Nobel laureate Milton Friedman, that a business has only one responsibility: economic performance." Drucker maintains that economic performance is the *first*, but not *only* responsibility of a corporation. He adds that accepting social responsibility for not only shareholders but customers, employees, and communities as well will be a primary task for *all of us* in the very different world he believes we are creating.[17]

While some of Friedman's associates in Chicago have recently begun talks with the Vatican, Friedman once reviewed the important economic pastoral letter from Pope John Paul called *Centesimus Annus*, which went a long way toward embracing responsible capitalism. Echoing Pilate, Friedman concluded by writing: "But I must confess that one high-minded proposition, passed off as if it were a self-evident proposition, sent shivers down my back: obedience to the truth about God and man is the first condition of freedom. Whose 'truth'? Decided by whom?"[18]

Indicating that he prefers for God to stay in heaven and leave this world to economists, Friedman once told *Religion and Liberty*: "The growth and development of Britain and the United States and other advanced countries did not owe anything to organized religion . . . I am concerned that as of now the organized church is more likely to be an obstacle to the achievement of the right kind of economic institutions than it is to be a source of strength . . . The church tends to believe that is should exercise control not only over the spiritual realm but also over the material realm, and that's where all the difficulties arise."

Unfortunately, I often hear Judeo-Christian leaders quote Friedman's views as if they were gospel. In short, religious leaders should understand what even George Bernard Shaw knew when he said, "Whether you think Jesus was God or not, you must admit that he was a first-rate political economist." The traditional Judeo-Christian position has *always* been that "love thy neighbor as thyself" means personal responsibility *must* be balanced with social responsibility. If it is not, personal responsibility simply becomes a code word for taking care of number one.

The sign of the cross symbolizes the truth that we are to *love* God and our neighbor unconditionally. This love is the organizing force of the universe. By contrast, in the final sentence of *Atlas Shrugged*, Ayn Rand has her hero, John Galt, make the sign of the dollar over the world. It symbolizes her belief that the selfish *pursuit of money* should be the organizing force of the universe.

This is why Jack Kemp felt so uneasy about the idea that conservatives must choose between economics and cultural renewal. It is why so many Americans seem frustrated that our only political choice is between communists on the left and barbarians on the right. And it may be why Bill Bennett has written:

> The conservative agenda is politically dominant but fundamentally incomplete. Republicans eventually must stand for more than shifting the focus of funding from Washington to Sacramento. . . . Even if government directly undermined civic society, it cannot directly reconstruct it.[19]

There are few political solutions to moral problems. If there were, Jesus would not have fled when the people wanted to make him king.

THE CATTLE ON A THOUSAND HILLS

The secret of success is giving, not getting. Those who are grown up give. The immature do not. It is wise to practice giving in every area of life.
                                                    Sir John M. Templeton

Altruism is incompatible with freedom, with capitalism and with individual rights. . . . No man, neither Negro or white, has any claim to the property of another man.

Ayn Rand

Arianna Huffington is a senior fellow at the Progress and Freedom Foundation, a think tank often associated with Newt Gingrich. She heads its Center for Effective Compassion, which promotes private giving to replace the welfare state. She recently spoke on C-Span concerning the question "Can Conservatives Have a Social Conscience?" One of her primary contentions is that we Americans have grown selfish during recent years. Conservatives usually assume that as deep cuts are made in welfare, private giving will take up the slack. But will it?

Obviously, selfishness has been around since the fall of man. In the opening chapters of the Bible, Cain asks, "Am I my brother's keeper?" Many of us have consciences that remind us to do more for the needy of the world, and, personally, I hope we never lose that holy discomfort—for it means that some spiritual life remains in our hearts and souls.

So is Randist selfishness any different that Cain's? Yes. It is very different. As Nathaniel Branden wrote, "What is new is the Objectivist validation of the theory of individualism and the definition of a consistent way to practice it."[20] In simple terms, Rand's disciples now have a moral justification for the abandonment of their brothers. Perhaps for the first time in the history of civilized people, selfishness is considered a virtue rather than a moral failing.

Despite Rand's assertion that each of us possesses an absolute right to "our" own property, Judeo-Christianity has always maintained we are simply stewards of property that belongs to the true Owner. The laws spelled out by Moses allowed *limited* access to property that "belonged" to others (Deuteronomy 23:24–25). And though Jesus and his disciples were not property owners, they were *not* stealing as they plucked grain and were challenged about working on the Sabbath.

John Templeton's assertion that giving is more important than getting is a reminder that creating wealth must be balanced with its distribution. (Where would we be if after creating the world, God refused to share it with us?) With government shifting responsibility for the needy back to churches and individuals, that kind of thinking will be needed more and more. The *Wall Street Journal* has estimated that every church in America will need to raise between $200,000 and $300,000 annually to match the projected cuts in welfare spending.[21]

Nevertheless, Congressman Armey originated the effort to eliminate the tax deduction for charitable giving. (Remember the statistic about economists and giving?) The *Wall Street Journal* has said that most politicians are reluctant to eliminate it, but economist Armey "is willing to tackle colleges and churches by halting the deduction for charitable contributions."[22] "Tackle" strikes me as a most appropriate word here, since it denotes "stopping the progress of something." Unless humans suddenly become angels, eliminating those tax deductions will hardly encourage more private charity at a time when we are reducing welfare and aid to education. (Personally, I wonder if a 5% to 10% *tax credit*, which would be a dollar-for-dollar deduction against your federal taxes, might not be more effective in solving America's social and moral problems. It would free each of us to choose between personally caring for our neighbors or having the government do it for us, a somewhat biblical, and realistic, approach in my view. And it might bring us closer together as neighbors.)

I also thought it rather sad when the *Wall Street Journal* reported, "[Jack] Kemp declined to run [for president] after his incessant calls for Republicans to reach out to racial minorities drew lukewarm reactions from party activists."[23]

I have never been more embarrassed to call myself a religious conservative than at the conclusion of a Christian radio interview in which I discussed the South Shore Bank and Opportunity International. Both are voluntary, market-oriented efforts in which I have chosen to invest in order to help those with whom Jesus most closely identified. They do this not through welfare, which can unintentionally foster dependency, but by helping people help themselves, to build self-esteem and a future. After the show, several callers complained to the host for allowing a "liberal" on the air. I felt a tear fall from heaven.

So let me be as clear as I possibly can: you *can* advocate that our government run on a more fiscally conservative basis and *still* have a social conscience.

My second greatest embarrassment as a religious conservative may have been when Larry Burkett wrote:

> As cruel as it may sound, from the long-term perspective of the economy, it would be better to raise taxes on the poor than on the wealthy. It is only the wealthy—the people who have surplus

money—who are able to invest in industries that create the jobs and wages that make it possible for the poor to escape their poverty.[24]

Such thinking may have encouraged the libertarians to work to eliminate the Earned Income Tax Credit for the poor. In essence, rather than penalize the poor for working by reducing benefits, this program allows them to keep more of what they earn in the workplace. In a special section titled "American Survey: A Slap in the Face for the Working Poor," *The Economist* noted that then-governor Ronald Reagan first thought enough of that idea to advance it. When as president he signed its expansion in 1986, he thought it was "the best anti-poverty, the best pro-family, the best job-creation measure to come out of Congress." President Bush thought enough of it to expand it once again, with the endorsement of the conservative Heritage Foundation. And traditional conservatives like Jack Kemp have recently voiced support for reforming, not eliminating, the credit. So we might take note that *The Economist* quipped that when today's new "Republicans say they are not balancing the budget on the backs of the poor, that they are serious about work-based welfare reform, and that their tax policies are not skewed to favor the rich, think of the EITC and reach for the salt."[25]

THAT OLD DEVILISH PRIDE

This is the Humble Approach: To assume a realistic attitude before the Creator and admit that we are not the center of the universe. . . . Egotism is still our worst enemy. . . . Humility is the gateway of knowledge. . . . The question before us is whether theologians and religious scholars, clergy and laity, are also taking the humble approach.

Sir John M. Templeton

Humility is, of necessity, the basic virtue of a mystical morality; it is the only virtue possible to men who have renounced the mind . . . to gain the virtue of humility, one has only to abstain from thinking.[26]

Nathaniel Branden

John Templeton has written a personal theology, called *A Theology of Humility*, which is based on two verses from the Scriptures: "Moses was the most humble man on earth" and "Not my will, but thine be done." In part, it says, "The *Theology of Humility* does not encourage syncretism but rather an understanding of the benefits of diversity." In essence, John finds no need to mix his belief with the secular religions of either the left or the right. Yet true unconditional love for those secular humanists with whom he disagrees is an absolute tenet of his faith—exactly the kind of love that I, frankly, find to be the most difficult to achieve.

Still, I will admit that God still works in strange ways and all of us may have benefited from the diverse opinions that the objectivists and libertarians have brought to America's political economy, even if I don't fully understand them. I remember standing once in the dark, damp catacombs outside Rome. I wondered how the people of those days felt when they read Paul's letter that said the Roman authorities could serve only if God willed it and they should therefore be submitted to and obeyed (Romans 13). When my clients seem particularly worried and unhappy about the government, I encourage them to seriously reflect on this passage to honestly evaluate whether their mindset is closer to Paul's or Rand's.

Yet Paul traveled over the roads and shipping channels developed by the Roman authorities to spread his Good News throughout the Mediterranean and into Europe. Later, the Good News spread to the other continents of the world, including North America. Perhaps he knew what he was talking about after all. Perhaps we should just trust that God is indeed using political leaders—perhaps without their even knowing it—to further his kingdom.

Nevertheless, Ayn Rand, like Marx, was one more self-proclaimed prophet who denied the existence of a loving God—One who asked us to love others as he has loved us. Before she died, Rand wrote, "Today, the world is facing a choice: if civilization is to survive, it is the altruist morality that men have to reject."[27]

Let us hope there are enough of us who disagree with Ayn Rand. Forty years from now, I will hate to explain to a young person that the greatest challenge of my life was learning to love Ayn Rand—despite what she did to America's soul. Think of those young people for a moment as you reflect on these words from Bill Bennett:

> I think we have made enormous gains: material comforts, economic prosperity, and the spread of democracy around the world. Yet even with all of this, the conventional analysis is still that this nation's major challenges have to do with getting more of the same. But to look to any or all of them as the solution to what ails us is akin to assigning names to images and shadows, it so widely misses the mark. If we have full employment and greater economic growth—but our children have not learned how to walk in goodness, justice, and mercy, then the American experiment, no matter how gilded, will have failed.

ten

ACHIEVING TRUE SUCCESS

GOLDEN RULE:
Measure success with a single word—love

Success is nice and I've had some and enjoyed it, but—so what? It isn't sufficient reason to get up in the mornings. It's not good enough to live for. Success for me has been, essentially, getting invited to things I don't want to go to but like saying I went to. And one of the reasons for that is that I found I wasn't as drawn to and charmed by experience anymore—at least the kind of experience that is being at the party, the convention, in the hot-air balloon. All that now seemed mostly fine but basically overrated. Oddly enough, whenever I have been at the center of things—in the White House, at the party, in the studio—I would enjoy them and have a great time and notice things, but I would also think, and it wasn't only a detaching mechanism, a self-protecting way of not being there, I would also think: This is all an illusion. This is a lovely, tender illusion. We're all running around being busy and doing important things but this has nothing to do with anything. Up there God and the angels are looking down and laughing, and not unkindly. They just find us—touching and dizzy.

Peggy Noonan

*S*uccess. What is it? How do we find it? What does it mean for our country our world and our children?

As Solomon lovingly cautioned, we may chase money, power, and pleasure to make us feel successful, but we will still discover that it is chasing the wind.

And like Peggy Noonan, who as President Reagan's speech writer captured in words so many inspiring thoughts and was at the center of the attractions this world has to offer, many of us seem to be wandering back to the same place—the simple faith of our youth. It seems Solomon again bequeathed us a pearl when he wrote: "This only have I found: God made mankind upright, but men have gone in search of many schemes" (Ecclesiastes 7:29).

THE CIRCLES OF FAITH

The Protestant Reformation released the great surge of individualism that created the modern West, including what we now call capitalism and democracy. But for the first two centuries after the Reformation, this new dynamo of individualism operated inside a still generally accepted body of Christian discipline. Then, in the eighteenth century, the era of the Enlightenment, this sort of discipline began to break down. People started to believe that the human mind alone was capable of answering any question. Humankind was self-sufficient.

The Economist

After fifteen years of studying Sir John Templeton's life and work, I am convinced that the true secrets of his success are that he has held to a simple belief and has lived that simple faith as he has journeyed through the complicated worlds of Yale, Oxford, and international finance.

Meditate for a moment on these thoughts from the interview *Forbes* conducted with John in 1978. Reflect on how they might have enriched American life during the economic excesses of the eighties and the political excesses of the nineties. Consider the spiritual peace they might bring to those of us who have grown skeptical, perhaps even cynical, of life in our modern world:

> This extraordinary man believes that successful investing is a product of a person's overall relationship to life, to the universe. He explains why religion is so important to successful investing: "Religious views are important to whatever anyone does—investing, writing articles, anything. How you see yourself in relation to others and your Creator, why, it's *the* most important thing that there is because you think most clearly only if you are at peace with yourself and your Creator."

> Unlike most of us, Templeton is at peace with himself. He has sorted things out. He believes that God created and is creating the universe; and that while this is no license to do nothing in life, neither should we continually question whether our bosses or spouses are double-crossing us, say, or whether the market will go to 400 or 4000. This gives Templeton extra mental energy to make and stand by his decisions.

> But while he is no dogmatist, neither has he any use for "humanists," by which he means people who consider man, not God, to be the center of the universe: "Many, many brilliant people hold to humanist viewpoints, which is one reason why the world is in so much trouble now. Pass a new law. Spend more money. Let government direct your life. All these are humanist dictates, showing that too many people are relying on human beings and governments rather than God for their welfare."

> Nor does he respect the skeptics—those who doubt everything. Templeton trusts the universe and his own judgment because he trusts in God.

According to some studies, 90% of all Americans say they believe in God. A majority of us attend church fairly often. Yet these studies also say that during the past ten years, the number of us who think biblically and live as "serious Christians" has declined from 12% to 6%.[1] Though this trend may be reversing, many of us could still be enriched by the way John has connected his beliefs to the way he lives.

CONNECTING WITH SUCCESS

Islam ignores the frontier that most people draw between man's inner life and his public actions, between religion and politics. It may be the last such idea the world will see. Or it may, on the contrary, prove to be the force that persuades other people to rediscover a connection between day-to-day life and a moral order. . . . The distinguishing feature of Islam is its belief not only that man's day-to-day life is surrounded by an invisible life but that the two have to be kept in connection with each other. The West held the same combinations of beliefs until not long ago; but at some time during the present century, most people in Europe and many Americans, have ceased to make such a connection.

The Economist

It would upset most Christians and Jews I know to suggest that God might use Muslims to remind us of the important truths outlined in the previous quote. But the *Economist* was right. My personal experience is that we can all find riches by reconnecting the various fragments of our divided lives.

When, in the eighties, I considered attending seminary, most people were stunned. Hadn't I found success already? I had an executive position with a major corporation. I had the corner office overlooking the bay. I made lots of money. I had cars, boats, and other toys America seems to value. And I was a lay leader of my local church. But what most people didn't know was that I was anxious, angry, and unhappy. I was fleeing my world rather than going to seminary.

My denomination's psychologist conducted a battery of tests. One measured whether I journeyed through the world by thinking or feeling. The test said I was over on the feeling side. The psychologist said I struck him as a thoughtful fellow so the test was probably wrong. I have always hoped both the test and the psychologist were right.

We modern humans commonly believe that we think with our minds and feel with our hearts. Psychologists have developed a test to measure our ability to think. They call it IQ—intelligence quotient. But only recently have some psychologists started to speak of EQ—emotional quotient—that measures our ability to think emotionally.

They suggest that those who can connect their hearts and minds not only show great intelligence but use that intelligence in caring ways. Emotional intelligence keeps us from becoming "evil geniuses," gifted with the power of reason but using it for our own selfish ends. The new theories of EQ tell us this more integrated approach can help lead us to higher probability of finding success.[2]

But in the eighties, I knew all that. I felt I was successfully combining my business and my emotions for the good of as many people as possible. So why was I still anxious and unhappy?

John Templeton led me to the answer. While mind and heart may be connected and produce material success, true success comes only when your soul is in the loop too. That is spiritual success, the kind you can feel on the inside. Templeton's gift to me was to point me toward that kind of success, and my gift, in return, has been to make the admittedly difficult journey in that direction, to bring not only mind and heart but soul into the world of finance.

TRUE, JOYOUS, COMPLETE SUCCESS

Life for most people in the West is in many ways far more enjoyable than it was a century ago, before farm laborers and factory hands had become a vast new middle class. But now this new middle class is starting to suspect that life has suddenly become more brutal and more hazardous.

This is why the West must find a way of putting individual initiative, the necessary diving-force of progress, within a shaping moral order. Otherwise, the history books will record that the people of the West woke up during the twenty-first century to discover that the pursuit of efficiency is not the same as the achievement of a happy life.

The Economist

Some of the most profound stories in the Scriptures are so simple that you can read them for years and yet miss their wisdom. Luke 10:38–42, for me, is one such story. When Jesus visits Bethany, Mary takes advantage of his presence to sit quietly at his feet and connect with the Master. In contrast, Martha scurries around being productive and efficient. As I reflect on this story, I wonder what Martha was doing that was so important—and I marvel that nearly everyone I know makes the same mistake. In the crush of our busyness, we forget to simply connect with the love of the universe.

The secular religions of Marx and Rand specialized in the kind of distracting busyness that blinded them to spiritual things. Furthermore, they are simply wrong about the nature of our life and world. As Templeton once said: "Almost everything is temporary; life, deeds, business. What matters is to learn God's purposes and to connect with them. Everyone asks why we are here. Well, maybe it's to learn, to grow spiritually."[3]

Marx failed because he was wrong about human nature. People who are truly human will never allow government elites to do their thinking and caring for them—especially at the expense of the needs of the soul in this life or the next.

Ayn Rand will likely fade from people's memories for much the same reason. She could not grasp that a human being is much more than a rational mind. The true human being has a heart and soul that needs to love God and neighbor more than any material possession. Any approach to political economy—or personal financial management—that denies these twin needs is unlikely to be anymore successful than communism was.

Someone once said: if we aren't socialists by the time we are thirty, we should check our hearts, and if we aren't capitalists by the time we are forty, we should check our heads. But baby boomers in particular should note that there is another part of the journey toward Truth: if we are not loving stewards by the time we are fifty, we should check our souls.

I believe this progression—from heart to mind to soul—is more than just personal. I think entire nations make the same journey. Much of the formerly communist and socialist world has matured and embraced the freedoms of democratic capitalism. I am sure they will experience many of the same growing pains that plagued America from the sixties to the eighties. But America seems to have matured to the point at which it is now desperately seeking its soul. I pray that this focus on caring for God and our neighbor—what I call "stewardism"—will prove to be the much sought alternative to government-centered socialism and self-centered capitalism.

For these reasons, I believe God-centered John Templeton—unlike Karl Marx and Ayn Rand—correctly understands the nature of the universe, the world, and the human condition. If you don't believe it, just look at a few of the people who have received his now famous Templeton Prize for Progress in Religion.

In 1973, he honored Mother Teresa. With the heart of Christ, she loves her neighbors enough to freely and joyously choose the materially sacrificial life. She is to be treasured by those of us who have set our hearts on riches that are all too temporary in nature.

John later awarded another prize to Michael Novak, a former columnist for *Forbes* and a fellow at the American Enterprise Institute. With the mind of Christ, Novak's work has created a treasure of the "shaping moral order" and spiritual principles that democratic capitalism needs if it is to truly enrich the lives of our children in the coming millennium.

John was right to award a more recent prize to Charles Colson, a man who has made an astounding personal journey from senior White House adviser to prison inmate to a servant of God. With the soul of Christ, he accepted the Prize by using these golden words within his speech:

> Four great myths define our times—the four horsemen of the present apocalypse. The first myth is the goodness of man. The second myth is the promise of coming utopia. The third myth is the relativity of moral values. And the fourth myth is radical individualism.
>
> The four horsemen of the present apocalypse lead us away from the cloud and fire of God's presence into a barren wilderness. This is the lesson of centuries; that ordered liberty is one of faith's triumphs.
>
> And yet, western cultural and political elites seem blinded by modernity's myths to the historic civilizing role of Christian faith. These elites seek freedom without self-restraint, liberty without standards. But they find instead the revenge of offended absolutes. Universities reject the very idea of truth, and we are shocked when the best and brightest of their graduates loot and betray.
>
> A generation of cultural leaders wants to live off the spiritual capital of its inheritance, while denigrating the ideals of its ancestors. It squanders a treasure it no longer values.

PANNING THE WATERS OF HEAVEN

Something significant is stirring in America's spiritual life. In America, unlike Europe, religious belief has strengthened down the years. The rise was remarkably smooth until the rebellious 1960s, when the numbers fell somewhat, prompting a 1966 Time cover story to ask provocatively, and prematurely, "Is God Dead?" A resurrection is now apparent.

The Economist

Forbes' interview with John Templeton concluded by saying: "Great genius is a mystery, incapable of being reduced to a formula or programmed into a computer. John Templeton has such genius. You can analyze him and study what he does, but you can't emulate him."

We often talk about and admire successful philosophies, but we hesitate to live them. For that reason, I think the *Forbes* reporter was simply wrong. Of course, John Templeton lives life to his own high standards, and I cannot claim to have achieved the same standards for myself. But as an investment professional, I have in John Templeton a model to work toward in this complex world. And it has been most enriching.

Although few of us have had the education that John has been blessed with, it's worth noting that, although he studied economics at Yale and law at Oxford, no degrees were then offered in investment management. He gained his great wisdom after he had completed his formal education. Those of us who think our education was finished when we left school might be greatly encouraged by that. As Solomon said, "[Wisdom] is more precious than rubies; nothing you desire can compare with her" (Proverbs 3:15). Yet we need to remember that wisdom is different than information. Confusing the two is yet another defining characteristic of the Enlightenment mind.

Few of us will ever have John Templeton's decades of experience. But we do have something he never had: the example of his life. And it is not a terribly difficult life to learn from. Essentially, it has been built on a simple faith. When he has read the Scriptures over the years, he has simply connected with the inspired minds of the past. When he has prayed before making decisions, he has simply connected with the Great Mind. When he has practiced ethics in his money management, he has simply connected with his neighbors. And when he has given generously of his time, talent, and treasure, he has simply connected with the higher nature that exists in all of us.

We might treat his example like that of the Apostle Paul, who, while encouraging us to focus our attention on God, also asks us to learn from his own weakness and experience. It would seem most unprofitable to treat John's example as though it were a religious icon, protected behind bulletproof glass, as the article in *Forbes* seemed to suggest. Just as Paul used the commercial trade routes of his own day to spread the gospel, we might use our professional lives to do the same—much as John Templeton has done.

A SIMPLE, HUMBLE APPROACH

Sir John is more than a person. He is a philosophy and a discipline.
Jane Siebels-Kilnes, Ph.D., Senior Portfolio Manager,
Templeton Mutual Funds

As we ask, "How shall we then live?" most of us will never consciously reject traditional religion by claiming God is dead and turn to secular religions like Marxism or Objectivism. Yet we may fail to achieve the success God wants for us by continuing to live as though God doesn't care or God is too weak to achieve his purposes on earth, which, by the way, was John Wesley's definition of a true atheist.

If you feel life has grown more complicated than it needs to be, you might try this exercise. Spend several weeks trying to decipher Marx's *Das Kapital* and Rand's *Atlas Shrugged*. Then spend a couple of hours with the simple parables of Jesus. You may discover that life simply isn't as complicated as most of us make it these days.

Jesus made successful living as simple as *loving* God, your neighbor, and yourself.

Do you remember the story of Zacchaeus? He was a wealthy but little man. When the crowds gathered around Jesus, he climbed a sycamore tree to see. But Jesus asked him to come down to earth. Then Jesus simply—absolutely—loved him. Zacchaeus responded by making amends with his neighbors and giving one-half of what he owned to the poor. The Scriptures do not say he made grand promises to go to church each week. They don't say he promised to preach to others or to reform the government.

They simply say he connected with God, his neighbor, and his own soul. His love, in other words, was evidenced by a humbled inward attitude toward wealth. He was set free to enrich the materially, mentally, and spiritually poor. Climbing down out of that tree that elevated him above his neighbors and perhaps himself, and connecting with God proved to be the best investment he could make. For Jesus said he found true success on that day. Not one day. But that day.

Simple.

A FINAL TREASURE TO ENRICH YOUR MIND AND SPIRIT AND POINT YOU TO TRUE SUCCESS

Wealth, for the successful person, however, has a purpose that goes beyond mere accumulation. Otherwise material goods can actually careen out of control, turn on their possessors, and ultimately destroy them.

Unlike Midas, whose wealth exerted a negative force, Templeton had a positive solution to the "problem" of money; he would use his material gains in a way that would benefit others. His attitude toward his worldly success involved a sense of stewardship, a belief that what you have is not actually yours but is held in trust for the good of all humanity.

John Templeton has never been satisfied to be merely wealthy. He has also worked hard, studied hard, and always prayed to be loving and giving. For him, these are the qualities that make for success. Through the years, he has kept to a great vision and a high standard—to seek the original, the spiritual, and the love and understanding of God.

Therein lies his success.

The Templeton Plan

I have been in a lot of investment firms during my twenty years on Wall Street. I have usually noticed that their walls are covered with graphs of a soaring Dow Jones Industrial Average, pictures of gushing oil wells, and sketches of towering real estate projects. Each symbolizes our preoccupation with the material riches to be gained in this world.

But the walls of John Templeton's headquarters are covered with framed butterflies. Butterflies are the ancient Christian symbol that when we die to the fear and greed of our human natures, we are transformed into the most beautiful of creatures. Despite all the awards, accolades, magazine covers, and television shows, it is really this ancient symbol that captures the essence of Sir John's success.

Successful investing can be simple. The lessons are easy as long as you have spiritual foundations and faith in the future. Remember, my ABCs of investing are ethics, prudence, and performance. Value ethics—in the companies you invest in, the companies you deal with when investing, including any investment counselor. Be prudent—choose your investments and your investment experts carefully. Study performance—check the record of any investment before you buy.

Finally, John Templeton taught me patience. Stay in for the long run. Patience smoothes out the highs and lows along the journey to success.

And have faith. If you have taken your steps carefully, you can relax, leaving your investments to grow so that years later you will have the added wealth to use for good, useful purposes.

Simple.

Notes

Chapter One: Pessimism Is Not a Virtue

1. *World Monitor* (February 1993).
2. *The Economist* (January 18, 1992).
3. The original version of this story, if you haven't guessed, can be found in the Bible—Numbers 13.
4. "The Humble Approach," *Possibilities* (Summer 1986).
5. *The Wall Street Journal* (November 24, 1995).

Chapter Two: Count Your Blessings

1. *The Wall Street Journal* (January 8, 1996), 1.
2. *The Economist* (November 25, 1995).
3. *The Wall Street Journal* (November 12, 1994).
4. *The Economist* (January 13, 1996).
5. *Christianity Today* (July 17, 1995), 26.
6. Louis Rukeyser, mailing to potential subscribers (June 29, 1995).
7. *The Limbaugh Letter* (January 1994).
8. *The Washington Post* (appeared in Syndicate Form, October 1994).
9. *Empower America Newsletter* (winter 1995).
10. *The Wall Street Journal* (October 19, 1994).
11. *The Economist* (September 11, 1993, and February 4, 1995).
12. *The Wall Street Journal* (July 23, 1993).
13. *The Wall Street Journal* (October 26, 1993).
14. George Will, "Critics Are Dealing with the Past," *Sarasota Herald-Tribune* (August 28, 1995).

Chapter Three: The National Debt and Your Future

1. *The Economist* (June 10, 1995).
2. *The Wall Street Journal* (November 18, 1994).
3. *The Economist* (January 7, 1995).
4. *Reader's Digest* (August 1995).
5. *The Wall Street Journal* (February 17, 1994).
6. *The Economist* (January 6, 1996).
7. *Outstanding Investor Digest* (February 8, 1990).
8. *Victory*, Peter Schweizer.
9. *The Economist* (July 8, 1995), 99.

10. *The Wall Street Journal* (November 18, 1994).

11. *The Economist* (December 23, 1995), 11.

12. Pat Robertson, *The New Millennium*, 244.

13. Larry Burkett, *The Coming Economic Earthquake*, 115.

14. Pat Robertson, *The New Millennium*, 245.

15. *Business Ethics* (November/December 1994), 21.

16. *The Wall Street Journal* (April 24, 1995).

17. *The Economist* (November 4, 1995).

18. *The Economist* (August 19, 1995).

19. *The Wall Street Journal* (July 31, 1995).

20. *The Wall Street Journal* (August 17, 1995).

21. *The Economist* (May 13, 1995).

22. *The Economist* (November 4, 1995).

23. "Budget Baselines, Historical Data and Alternatives for the Future," The Bush Administration.

24. Larry Burkett, *Planning for Retirement*, 175.

25. *Forbes* (July 20, 1992), 33.

26. *The Economist* (February 26, 1994), 74.

27. *Forbes* (July 19, 1993), 53.

28. *The Wall Street Journal* (November 9, 1994).

29. *Christianity Today* (August 14, 1995), 25.

Chapter Four: Find Safety in Numbers

1. *World Monitor* (February 1993).

2. *The Economist* (February 25, 1995), 18.

3. *Forbes* (February 28, 1994), 132.

4. *Morningstar* (July 21, 1995).

5. *The Limbaugh Letter* (date unknown).

6. *Forbes* (August 28, 1995), 172.

7. *The Wall Street Journal* (August 18, 1995).

Chapter Five: The Creative Uses of Money

1. The Franklin Funds acquired the Templeton Funds a few years ago. Though they largely continue to focus on different aspects of investing, they could basically be considered one fund group for purposes of switching among funds, etc. Franklin has long been known as a domestic stock and bond management firm while Templeton has been known as an international stock firm.

2. Special to the *Washington Post*, Sarasota *Herald Tribune* (August 13, 1995).

3. *The Economist* (June 17, 1995), 105.

4. *Fortune* (April 6, 1992).

5. *People* (February 23, 1987).

Chapter Six: The Power of Patience

1. *World Monitor* (February 1993).
2. Michael T. Jacobs, *Short-Term America.*
3. *Morningstar* (August 7, 1992).
4. Norman Zadeh, "Rules for Investors," *Barrons* (December 17, 1990).
5. *The Wall Street Journal* (May 17, 1990).
6. *Forbes* (July 20, 1992).
7. *Mutual Fund Market News*, Dalbar Study (January 26, 1994).
8. Forbes (February 12, 1996).
9. *Morningstar* (August 10, 1990, and July 23, 1993).
10. *Forbes* (October 18, 1993), 43.
11. *The Bond Buyer* (February 21, 1995).

Chapter Seven: Whom Can You Trust?

1. *Forbes* (December 6, 1993), 275.
2. *Forbes* (July 20, 1992), 339.

Chapter Eight: Investing for Good

1. *Business Ethics* (November/December 1994).
2. Peggy Noonan, *Life, Liberty and the Pursuit of Happiness*, 205.
3. C. S. Lewis, *Mere Christianity*, 106.
4. Edmund A. Opitz, *Religion and Capitalism*, 34.
5. *Forbes* (August 28, 1995), 15.
6. *The Economist* (May 6, 1995).
7. *Worth* (December/January 1996), 32.
8. *Forbes* (December 4, 1995), 256.

Chapter Nine: Money, Morality, and a New Millennium

1. *The Economist* (December 25, 1993), 21–26.
2. *Worth* (May 1995).
3. *Barrons* (November 30, 1992), 23.
4. *The Wall Street Journal* (May 24, 1995).
5. E. J. Dionne, "Libertarians Seek a Harsh Utopia," Sarasota *Herald Tribune* (December 12, 1994).
6. Pat Robertson, *The New Millennium*, 254.
7. *The Wall Street Journal*, "Conservative Coalition Holds Firm," (February 13, 1995).
8. *The Wall Street Journal*, editorial page (September 5, 1995).
9. *The Wall Street Journal* (October 11, 1995), A2.
10. *The Economist* (November 26, 1994).
11. *TV Guide* (August 6, 1994), 20.
12. Ayn Rand, *The Virtue of Selfishness*, 54.

13. *The Wall Street Journal* (June 23, 1995).

14. George F. Will, "Easing the Welfare Wagon's Load," Sarasota *Herald-Tribune* (September 14, 1995).

15. David Broder, "Call Armey the GOP Scriptwriter," Sarasota *Herald Tribune* (June 21, 1995).

16. "Me! Me! Me!" *Forbes*, (September 12, 1994), 94.

17. Peter Drucker, *Post-Capitalist Society*, 101.

18. *National Review*, Special Supplement (date unknown), 2–4.

19. "Moving Beyond Devolution," *The Wall Street Journal*, (September 5, 1995).

20. Ayn Rand, *The Virtue of Selfishness*, 158.

21. *The Wall Street Journal* (November 7, 1995).

22. *The Wall Street Journal* (January 31, 1995).

23. "Growth Vs. Thrift," *The Wall Street Journal*, A10.

24. *The Coming Economic Earthquake*, Revised Edition, 10.

25. *The Economist* (July 8, 1995).

26. Ayn Rand, *The Virtue of Selfishness*, 44.

27. Ayn Rand, *The Virtue of Selfishness*, 39.

Chapter Ten: Achieving True Success

1. *Christianity Today* (September 11, 1995), 4.

2. You can read more about "E.Q." in the October 2, 1995, edition of *Time* magazine or the book *Emotional Intelligence* by Dr. Daniel Goleman, (New York: Bantam, 1995).

3. Orlando *Sun-Sentinel* (January 9, 1994).